CL16

Gloucestershire

COUNTY COUN

Items should be returned to any Gloucest
on or before the date stamped. Books wh'
be renewed in person, by lett
084⁵ 230 54⁻

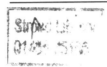

MANOLO BLAHNIK

MANOLO BLAHNIK

COLIN McDOWELL

CASSELL&CO

'Manolo Blahnik — the name has the magic of precious things: shoes like jewels — is the best known shoemaker in the world. He belongs next to Picasso, Lorca and Almodovar as representing the Spanish genius at its greatest.'

GUILLERMO CABRERA INFANTE

INTRODUCTION: This is less a conventional biography than an examination of the roots and inspirations of a man who has long been acknowledged as foremost in his field. It is also a chronicle of the steps that led him to that point but, again, it is not a conventional tale taking the reader logically from one moment to the next. It is more a thing of fits and starts, enthusiasms and joys, dislikes and objections: neither conventional, nor, except in the broadest of terms, strictly chronological.

What I have attempted is to conjure the spirit of a man whose mind moves like quicksilver, who flies across the years like Ariel, stopping at points and places where his imagination and memory are, temporarily, halted. I have spent two marvellously invigorating years following Manolo — from London to Bath to Milan to New York. He has never failed to entertain and amuse — but he has done more. As the months rolled by and the tape recordings piled up, it became apparent that there are two Manolo Blahniks: one as light and rich as a perfect plum soufflé; another, much more serious, intellectual and inclined to dark thoughts. It is Blahnik's triumph and tragedy that he has perfected the former to

the point where it almost totally eclipses the latter: it is the entertainer who appeals — and who, indeed, is pushed forward by Blahnik himself — to the detriment of the thinker, educated in and aware of a wide range of subjects and cultures. Manolo Blahnik is all spirit. He has total recall of the atmosphere and mood of moments going back almost fifty years, but ask him for a precise date and he panics immediately. The Manolo mind recalls only that which is of interest to it. Dates and names are definitely not his concern. Ask him about the colour of a woman's dress or the smell of her perfume and his eyes sparkle with the joy of recall. Try to pin him down even to something as broad as a year in which something of importance happened and he shies backward, eyes rolling like an Arab stallion frightened by a lion in a painting by Stubbs.

When Manolo and I first talked of the project, his extreme modesty and insecurity made him inclined to say no. 'Who would want such a book?' he asked, genuinely bewildered. 'A few Ukrainian art students, maybe?' This diffidence has been with him throughout. Originally, I had planned to talk to the many friends

What I have attempted is to conjure the spirit of a man whose mind moves like quicksilver, who flies across the years like Ariel, stopping at points and places where his imagination and memory are, temporarily, halted. I have spent two marvellously invigorating years following Manolo – from London to Bath to Milan to New York. He has never failed to entertain and amuse – but he has done more. As the months rolled by and the tape recordings piled up, it became apparent that there are two Manolo Blahniks: one as light and rich as a perfect plum soufflé; another, much more serious, intellectual and inclined to dark thoughts.

and admirers whom Manolo Blahnik has gathered to him over a highly successful career, but the more I came to know him the more convinced I became that, with one or two exceptions, the story did not need the comments of others. One of those exceptions, Manolo's sister, Evangelina, who is so close to him, felt from the outset that this book should and must be about him alone. She sees herself as an executor and facilitator of his ideas and nothing more. In this, she is wrong. She is a crucial cog in the creative and commercial equation but, at her wish, I have not interviewed her for this book.

Manolo's words were clearly going to be enough, in any case. They have taken some unravelling. To give one example of what makes being with him so endearing but often exhausting: about a year ago, we talked of Sicily, a romantic place to which we both respond. Our discussion was in the context of southern European architecture in general and we'd ranged over Italy, Spain and Portugal. I then changed the subject and asked him which was his favourite room. He replied instantly, describing a room in La Granja, in Sicily. I was stumped. Here was a building I could not recall as being there. We went on, however, and it was only later, when I was transcribing the tapes, that I realized that, with all the lightning-fast verbal legerdemain that characterizes the conversation of the multilingual Blahnik, he had elided two countries. With the vast store of knowledge that bubbles below all his cultural commentaries he was thinking of El Real Sitio de la Granja de San Ildefonso in Segovia in Spain but was also recalling, subconsciously, the influence it had exerted on Caserta, the palace built outside Naples by Charles III in emulation of Versailles. It is this dragonfly crisscrossing beneath the surface of his words that makes any conversation with Manolo Blahnik so pleasurable but also so challenging. He is not a man to talk to if you're feeling mentally tired.

I have interviewed most of the great fashion creators of the last twenty-five years and many have surprised me with the breadth of their knowledge, but none has fascinated as much as Manolo Blahnik. I hope this book will go some way to capturing for the general reader the unique essence of the man, which has lead to his pre-eminence, both social and professional, and made him loved and admired by all in the fashion world.

THE ENCHANTED GARDEN

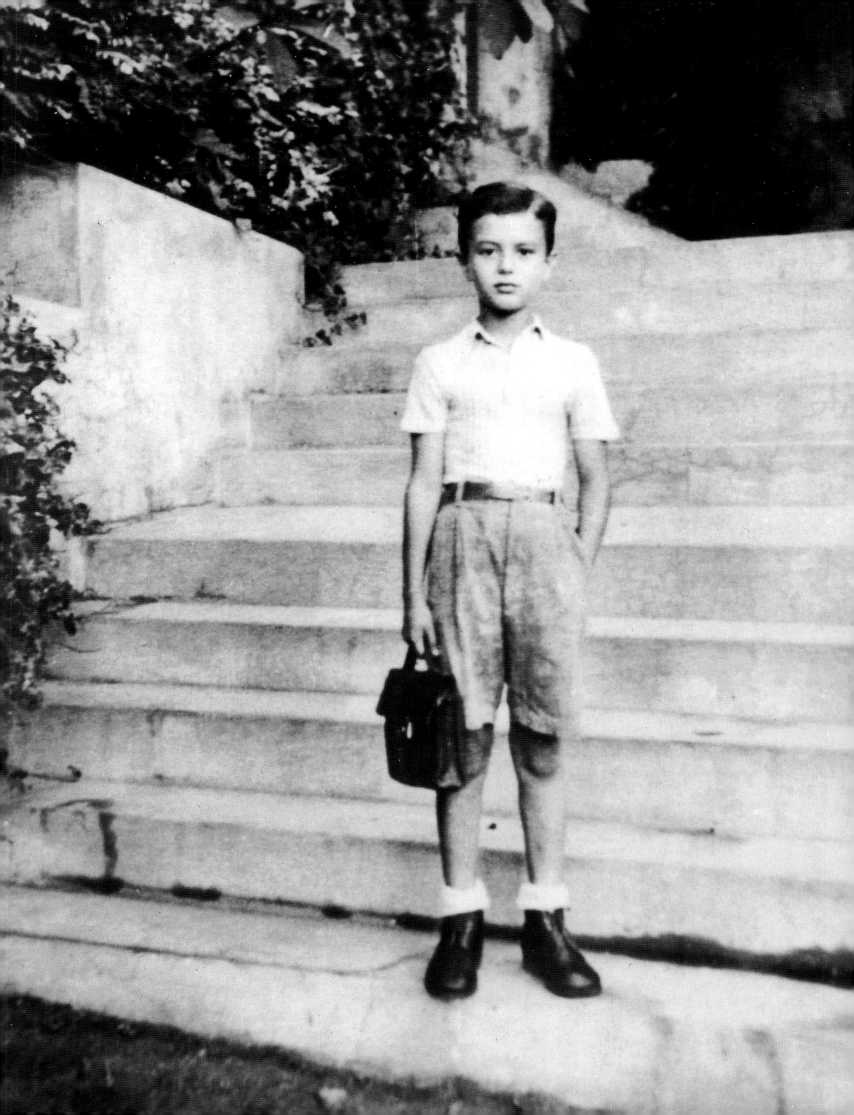

Left: Manolo, aged six, ready for his piano lesson with his music teacher, Don Sebastian. The routine of repetitive practice and Don Sebastian's tough discipline had a lasting effect on his young pupil. Even today the sound of the classical piano takes Manolo back to his schoolboy lessons.

Right: Manolo with his mother on the beach opposite the family home, photographed in 1944. The distant war in Europe made the Canary Islands feel more remote than ever by interrupting and delaying sea communications with Europe and the Americas.

'The number of shoemaker-intellectuals is impressive,' writes Eric Hobsbawm in his collection of essays *Uncommon People*, pointing out that shoemakers have long been known for their radicalism. It is interesting that one of the twentieth century's great political and intellectual commentators views shoemakers in this way. Neither he nor anybody else would make such a claim for other workers in the world of fashion and clothing. Intellectuality is not a quality often associated with couturiers or fashion commentators, any more than it is with milliners or make-up artists. What is it that makes the craftsman who works in shoes more likely to be a well-read thinker than most other workers in the fashion world?

Historically, shoemakers have always been known for the breadth of their reading and the openness to intellectual stimuli which it brings. Since medieval times, they have been craftsmen with a high level of literacy and great political awareness. Their guilds have been a sword in the flesh of emperors and kings, burghers and churchmen, in their refusal to conform to attitudes they felt were clearly wrong and in their determination not to maintain the status quo if it worked against a common good. Shoemakers were radicals, often revolutionaries. The place they hold in the long, slow struggle for democracy is an honoured one.

It is against such a background that modern shoemakers must be measured. Today they are unlikely to be political revolutionaries, but they can be relied upon to have a level of intelligence that makes them sharply aware of the world around them and conscious of many things beyond the narrow confines of fashion.

Theirs is, after all, an entirely practical trade. The most beautiful shoe has no meaning if it cannot be worn in safety and comfort. When shoes have high heels, the situation becomes more crucial. The difference between a good high-heeled shoe, which can be worn all day in comfort, and one which strains the calf muscles, pinches the foot and is tiring to wear is obvious to the wearer but is, in fact, a subtle equation in the design and making process that requires experience and knowledge to get right. Shoemaking can be claimed to be, if not quite a feat of intellect, then at least an intellectual exercise involving a mind that must be practical but not prosaic, a mind that has understood the basic science of the trade, thus enabling it to play with many variations to create a shoe of beauty and originality which works on an everyday level. The number of shoemakers who have this gift is small. One who most certainly has is Manolo Blahnik, the world's most creative shoemaker at the beginning of the new millennium, and the man who has comfortably led the field for the past twenty years.

The child is father to the man and in no case is this more obvious than that of Manolo Blahnik. The moods of the man were captured in 1977 by Michael Roberts, then an acquaintance of Blahnik's but not yet the close friend he has since become. In *The Sunday Times*, where he was then a fashion writer, Roberts described Blahnik, already a successful *bottier* with a high creative and social profile in London, as he galvanized his chichi little Chelsea shoe shop – all overblown flower arrangements and artistically arranged footwear. 'Customers constantly reel back as

the designer dashes about, chivying his assistants, commenting on the latest *Vogue*, and speaking volubly on the telephone to all his friends, from pal Bianca Jagger to his mother. "I used to be much worse, but now I'm much calmer", says Blahnik after a particularly heated moment.'

Brief as it is, Roberts's piece is telling in the details he picks up: the excitement tinged with panic; the instant reaction to stimulus; the nervous energy and, to use Manolo's own phrase, 'the verbal vomit' which makes him a nonstop, high-octane talker, as if he could not cope with a conversational vacuum. Roberts goes on to quote two comments that sum up the character of Manolo Blahnik. At one point the designer says, 'I don't trust anybody. I'm a perfectionist'. When asked by Roberts about his 'total lack of training in shoe design', he jokes, laughing ironically, 'I didn't need it because I've got the best taste in the world.' Insecurity and suspicion on one hand, confidence and courage on the other: to discover where such a volatile cocktail was mixed, it is necessary to go back to Manolo's childhood and early years, crucially formative of the man to come and far from conventional.

Manolo Blahnik was born in Santa Cruz de la Palma, in the Canary Isles off the Moroccan coast of North Africa, on November 27, 1942. One of the smaller and more far-flung of the island group, Santa Cruz moved slowly when Manolo was a small boy. Everything, including people, travelled by boat. There was no mass air travel and none of the tourism which has now overrun the islands. There was no television, although there were three picture palaces in Santa Cruz that were to exert an enormous and lifelong influence on Blahnik. His family were in the banana business, still the staple crop of the islands in the late forties and the fifties. The *finca* where they lived was outside the village, not remote – 'although it was a very small island, we had tiny roads and a few cars' – but idyllic. 'Our property had no neighbours apart from my grandfather's house. It was just bananas, the sea and us. I'll always remember the marvellous smell after a rainstorm, that subtropical smell of bananas and the lemon and orange trees which lined the plantation. It was a sort of paradise.'

The Canaries in the early fifties were like many remote places – grand Irish estates miles from Dublin or remote hill-towns in Umbria – moving to a rhythm behind that of the rest of the world. Until commercial air links were established in the sixties, life was, in essence, still that of the thirties for the middle classes and even further back for ordinary workers. It was gracious for people like Manolo's family, successful, well-off and established landowners, and remarkably formal. There were servants, a good social life and a surprising cultural one, also. The great Russian ballerina Anna Pavlova danced in Santa Cruz Tenerife and opera singers from Spain and Italy frequently visited. Surprisingly, Manolo recalls it as a distinctly Anglo-Saxon culture. The English used to winter there, often staying for months. They included Winston Churchill and Christopher Isherwood, both of whom had houses in the Canary Islands. In the summer, families came from Madrid for their holidays: 'I think what attracted them was that they

thought it was so remote, but we weren't that remote. We were quite near to Europe, after all, even by boat.'

The Blahnik family was not typical of most on the island because Manolo's mother had married outside the close-knit groups of her social circle, at the scandalously early age of eighteen. Manolo's father was Czechoslovakian, and met his future wife when the boat on which he was crossing the Atlantic from Hamburg put into port. It seems to have been love at first sight between the dark-eyed Spanish beauty and the green-eyed, blonde Viking type from Prague. She was marrying a man of some social and financial stature from an important Czech pharmaceutical family; he was marrying a woman remarkably attuned to cultural life far beyond the confines of the islands. It was a liaison sufficiently unusual for her father to have his prospective son-in-law checked out by the embassy before giving his consent.

Enan Blahnik had fallen in love not only with a woman but also with a place and a way of life. He joined the family banana business on his marriage in 1932. He also joined a secure and inward-looking society which must have seemed a strange contrast to Prague. When he was born in 1909, Czechoslovakia was still part of one of Europe's leading powers, the Austro-Hungarian empire. Manolo recalls being told that his father sang as a boy in the Cathedral of St Wenceslas. He also remembers proudly that his parents, true to the central European tradition of his father, had a Christmas tree brought from Czechoslovakia, making Manolo and Evangelina the only children on the island to have something different from a Spanish Christmas crib.

Both children were indulged. As Manolo says, 'They had to wait for ten years before I was born'. Evangelina was born twelve months later. The servants worshipped them and were frequently their allies against a family regime both formal and, at times, strict. Enan Blahnik was a disciplinarian and both he and his wife, Manuela, believed in the propriety of good behaviour. Politeness was a courtesy. Many people hearing Manolo Blahnik talk today consider his formality an affectation. Certainly, it is unusual in the fashion world, so casual and immediately intimate, to hear everyone in the Blahnik organization refer to people by their title. 'We created this shoe for Mr Galliano', an assistant will say. 'I admire Miss Wintour enormously', Manolo comments, formal even though Anna Wintour is a friend with whom, face to face, he is on Christian-name terms. Such courtesy, rather than fade since childhood, seems to have become something which means even more to Manolo and his sister now, and says much about how they view the world around them and their place within it.

Although, typically of his class at that time, Manolo spent much time with servants, he was expected to take part in the formal life of the *finca*. Always a bath and a nail inspection before dinner, even though he may have already showered three or four times

Left: Teenage poolside chic: Manolo and Evangelina pose by the family pool in the midday sun. The two siblings were – and remain – such close companions that it was almost inevitable that their parents would decide to separate them when it was time for them to go to university. Had they stayed together, Manolo says, they would have done nothing but enjoy themselves.

down at the poolside. Fastidiousness of person and dress were instilled at an early age and have remained, not just because it is a question of self-pride to appear looking correct but also because it would be a discourtesy to others not to do so. Manolo Blahnik simply does not know how to be informal anywhere but at the beach. Even at his home in Bath, wearing an old but beautiful turtleneck and cargo pants, his appearance always makes a statement about his refinement. His hair is always immaculately combed. 'Glued' is the word he uses for the preparation which keeps it under control. Asked if he ever leaves it *au naturel*, the reply is a shriek: 'Are you kidding? It would be totally wild. Beyond Beethoven on one of his bad days!' He washes it daily, alarmed at the idea of dandruff which he notices on other men's dark-suited shoulders – 'they remind me of St Petersburg under snow'.

Dinner parties were a nightmare for the boy, forcing him to play the formal role of the young man of the house, shaking hands with the guests and politely saying hello. The house was full of guests every summer. His father loved entertaining but Manolo now thinks his mother would have preferred to be in the garden, reading. Dinners meant dressing up and Manolo recalls his father's immaculate appearance. Before World War II, he had his clothes made in Prague, but subsequently had them tailored in Madrid, although, as Manolo says, 'he was always totally Czech'. Manolo recalls the morning room where most entertaining was done as

one of his favourites in the house. Painted in broad stripes of beige and bluey-grey, it had a clock from Prague which kept him awake at night, a grand piano and the huge ashtray obligatory in the fifties, when most sophisticated people smoked heavily.

It would have been very easy for the Blahnik family to turn its back on the world, especially at the time of the Spanish Civil War in 1936 or during World War II, but the cross-cultural mix of the marriage ensured that would not happen. Manolo thinks that, whoever his mother had married, her intellectual curiosity and need for cultural stimulus could only have been served by linking into a wider world. As it was, in the thirties his mother went to Prague, a sophisticated city with an elegant and formal middle and upper class where dress was an important part of the social equation. She loved the cultural opportunities it offered. She saw Smetana's *The Bartered Bride* four times on one visit. When she returned to the island she sometimes found it stifling but, in fashion terms, it was no backwater. Clothes were ordered from Madrid or the Gallerie Lafayette in Paris and Manolo remembers his mother saying that his grandmother ordered many items from Harrods' catalogue, to be made in London and shipped across.

During World War II, things were much more difficult, although his mother managed to keep up her standards of dress. She subscribed to US *Vogue*, *Glamour* and *Siluetas*, which were almost always a couple of months late, having been shipped via Cuba or

Right: A proud father with his teenage children, relaxing on the terrace of the family home. The pride was mutual: Manolo has always been very conscious of the Czech part of his heritage, even though the iron curtain made it impossible for him to visit his father's homeland for much of his life. In 1980 the two men made an emotional visit together to Prague, which Manolo considers one of Europe's most impressive and complete cities.

Left: For that all important first ball, Manolo wore black tie to reflect his parents' elegance and formality. He was sixteen at the time. His lifelong dedication to refinement in appearance and dress had its roots in his parents' insistence that fastidiousness in dress and manners was an essential courtesy to other people.

Right: Manolo with his mother in London in 1969, posing in front of a red MG that belonged to friends from Geneva.

Argentina. 'My mother always loved fashion', Manolo claims. 'She was extraordinary. She would look at the magazines and then talk to the seamstress who made her clothes, explaining how she should interpret the picture.' Manolo remembers that, even in the fifties, his mother had many of her clothes made locally by the woman who made his shirts and the pinafores he and Evangelina wore when they were young.

Shoes were very important to Manolo's mother. Frustrated by the restrictions imposed in the war when shoes arrived rarely – usually from Majorca – and were not up to her standards, she asked the local cobbler, Don Cristino, to teach her the rudiments of shoemaking. He provided the soles, including 'wedgies' hinged for walking, and she made the rest. Manolo remembers as a small boy watching her work with hammer and nails creating sandals of whatever fabrics she could lay her hands on, which included chiffon, caught with two knots, canvas and silk. 'I'm sure I acquired my interest in shoes generically', he claims, 'or at least through my fingers, when I was allowed to touch them as they were made.'

After the war Manolo's mother subscribed to many European magazines, including *Jour de France* and *Paris Match*, as well as US *Vogue*. Manolo was soon hooked on them and found the wait for the boats – often delayed by weeks in the winter – a great frustration. 'I was desperate for those magazines,' he recalls. He also waited eagerly for comic books and cartoons which came from Argentina. That said, his early life was not the normal life of a boy in the fifties. Educated at home and with few contacts with other boys of his age, he lived largely on the periphery of the adult world, listening to the gossip of the maids, learning how to get his own way in many different ways and living the rich imaginative interior life of a largely solitary child. As he explained to *Vanity Fair* almost forty years later, 'There were no friends… you had to build yourself games'. Manolo did so with his close friend Tito, the son of the *finca* caretaker.

The boy was adored by his parents, who had waited so long for a son and were thrilled to have him; by the servants, for the same sentimental reasons; and by his younger sister, with whom he has always had a very close relationship. Manolo learned how to manipulate in order to have his own way. He firmly denies that he was a 'mummy's boy' but admits, 'Whatever I am, I inherit from my mother. Evangelina is more like my father, *sportif* and business-minded.' Indeed, it is hard to imagine common ground between father and son, especially as the former lived for playing tennis and the latter hated all games, formal or informal.

Like many island societies, Santa Cruz was regularly taken by crazes, often spearheaded by new arrivals. Nobody welcomed such people more enthusiastically than Mrs Blahnik. 'My mother was ready and eager for every disaster,' Manolo laughs. 'Anybody who came to the islands and was doing something different instantly caught her imagination. "Oh", she'd say, "Would you mind if the children came along?" Every disaster we had to be part of. For example, there was a woman who took classes in Swedish gymnastics. The exercises were absolute torture but we had to go

along. I can tell you, we were victims of Swedish gymnastics! Three hours of exercise! Imagine!'

One reason Manolo hated gymnastics was that, like learning to play the piano, there was too much routine involved. His volatile mind, although not closed to discipline, has never been able to cope with repetitive things like practice. He especially disliked his music teacher. His mother's enthusiasm ensured that the children took singing and piano lessons. 'I had quite a good ear', he thinks now. 'But I had no gift for any of it. If I hear Chopin today, I go right back to those awful lessons. We had such a tough teacher. One day, shrieking, "No, you've done it wrong!" he brought a ruler down heavily across my hands. I was shocked but I look back now and think of it as rather a divine moment. So Hollywood!'

'I was a "cruel" child', he continues. 'I always loved black humour. Of course, for our parents, we had to be the best-behaved, best-dressed children on the island, but when my parents weren't around I remember that I could be quite naughty. But normally I was gentle. I used to love catching lizards – they're everywhere out there – and wrapping silver paper around them to make dresses. I also used to try to make little shoes for my dog and my pet monkey. By that time, I was obsessed by the Ballets Russes so I called them Diaghilev and Nijinsky.' It was all part of the fantasy world which children who live lonely lives create for themselves. I am reminded of the Brontës and the imaginary world they created for themselves to mitigate the remoteness of nineteenth-century life in the Yorkshire Dales in England. Such loneliness can be the forcing ground for the development of talents that more mundane and everyday lives do not develop.

Blahnik looks back on island life with fondness. 'It was very backward in many ways', he admits. 'In fact I guess it was in some respects at least sixty years behind the mainland. But I was a very happy child. Island life was totally uncomplicated. Sea and sun, basically. We had lots of summer companions, children who came from Cádiz and Madrid and would often stay for three or four months. The Prague side of our family was very important. Although the war stopped me going to Prague, my father's family came to see us.' Such easy communication ended abruptly in 1948 when Czechoslovakia was taken over by the Russians. Manolo recalls how his grandparents, visiting Santa Cruz, had to return immediately. 'All the servants were whispering, "Are they going back?" and the maids were crying. It was very sad. Then the iron curtain came down and my father couldn't even return until the mid-seventies, when things eased slightly.'

Manolo's parents realized it was time for him to break out of the narrow life of the Canary Islands. So he was sent to Geneva to study, whilst Evangelina went to Germany. It was a great wrench but both siblings now see how important it was to separate them. Not only did they not need companions when they were together, but they would not learn languages unless they were apart and forced to communicate with others. As Manolo admits, 'If we'd stayed together, we would have learned little and done nothing except enjoy ourselves.'

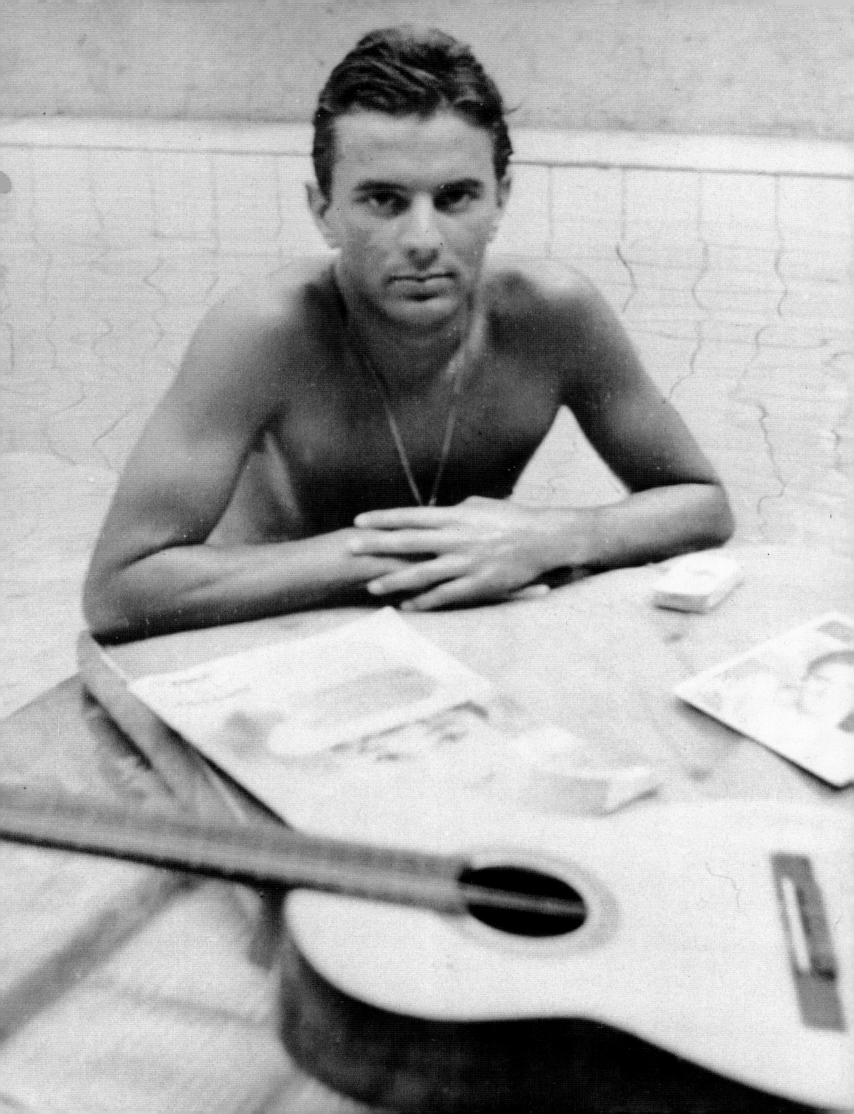

MEMORIES AND MOMENTS

'I was brought up with traditions and dignity, in the old-fashioned way. I don't think I could do anything without pride,' Manolo Blahnik contends, and there is no doubt that his mixed cultural antecedents have all brought that dignity to a rich fruition. Middle European, southern Mediterranean and British cultural references inform everything Blahnik does and has done since he was a schoolboy, and even before.

His mother, Manuela, was a voracious reader who devoured British and European literature in translation, as well as books in her native Spanish, and she shared her joy in reading with both her children from a very early age. Manolo recalls, for example, that the Canary Isles in the forties were no more immune from the hysteria swirling around Margaret Mitchell's *Gone With the Wind* than anywhere else. The book was translated into Spanish in 1942 and Manolo's mother read it to him as his goodnight story in bed. 'I was brought up with the Tarleton twins and Aunt Pittypat', he laughs. 'My mother read it to us every night, although she kept saying it was unsuitable. I can't have been more than four or five at the time.'

Bedtime reading was part of a remote but exceedingly eclectic education which went from Latin and Greek, taught by a woman Manolo claims was his favourite out of all the teachers and tutors who worked with him, through his father's obsession with the speeches and writings of Sir Winston Churchill to the English classics, such as Dickens. '*Little Dorrit*', he recalls with a shudder. 'How sad it was. I really couldn't bear it. *Great Expectations*. I really

couldn't bear the sadness. Of course, when I was younger it was Enid Blyton's Famous Five. My mother loved Mauriac, so my sister and I had to put up with him although neither of us found anything in him at all. I detested him and I still do. Torture! My mother read like mad and I suppose a lot of it was trash but I enjoyed it when she read for me. I grew up on translations from the sublime – Flaubert, for example – to the horrific: people like Cecil Roberts and Pearl S. Buck, although I do remember being very moved by *The Good Earth*. Later, my mother fell in love with Steinbeck, I remember.'

Manolo Blahnik's upbringing had a remarkably Anglo-Saxon flavour to it, although he points out that neither Czech nor Spanish writers were ever neglected. 'We were Quixote-ed to death, believe me,' he says. 'Both my parents were Anglophiles and, without really being aware of it at the time, I was brought up with a strong English cultural background. We took *The Illustrated London News*, for example. I suppose my education was an informal fusion of that, Spanish and Slav. I was very lucky to be given such a wide multicultural base. And I do feel very much a product of all this.'

What Blahnik's background gave him, which he now considers of crucial importance, were points of reference. He is not the kind of designer who searches for inspiration by working through old copies of fashion magazines, as many of his peers do, seeing such a referential approach as being too obvious, as is being in any way reactive to current fashion moods. Blahnik's creativity runs

much deeper. It is not a question of searching for surface stimuli. When he begins to sketch his ideas for a new season they will be informed by the subconscious layer of sophisticated knowledge which has been underpinned by his wide reading, his knowledge of art and architecture and his abiding love of the style of southern Europe.

By the time Blahnik was in his teens, he was directing his own reading and it concentrated on the cultural life which would prove to be his greatest stimulus: British upper-class mores of the between-the-wars years, 'the last time Britain was producing people of quality'. He was fascinated by Evelyn Waugh and Nancy Mitford; found Bloomsbury, Charleston and the Omega Workshop entrancing. He fell in love, above all, with the writings of Cecil Beaton — 'he was my idol' — reading and rereading every new volume of his diaries the moment they were issued. He was intrigued by biographies which revealed not only upper-class English ways of life but also social, intellectual and artistic attitudes. He was aware of Rex Whistler — 'I know every room and mural' — knew about Oliver Messel and was generally steeped in 'all the frivolities of British art, literature and writing in the twentieth century'. He identified with the eccentricities of the Sitwells, Lord Berners — who once claimed that his eyes were so kind that he had to wear dark glasses in Venice in order to deter the beggars — and Harold Acton. He admired them as much for their independence of view as for their knowledge so lightly, even flippantly, worn. As he grew up and matured, Blahnik displayed much the same attitudes.

It wasn't only England that this voracious appetite consumed. Blahnik also fell in love with numerous international figures of elegance. First on the list, again, would be Cecil Beaton, whose effetely sophisticated approach to dress appealed to the aesthetic young man. Its studied perfection masquerading as a casual degagé attitude intrigued him and he chose to emulate it — so successfully that he often features in lists of the 'world's best dressed men'. He felt much the same about the turn-of-the-century French dandy Robert de Montesquieu, who was painted by Sargent and Boldini. Looking back, he realizes that these sources were part of the cultural baggage he was amassing for his future life. 'I'm not an intellectual', he says, 'but I am a voracious observer of people's movements and attitudes in the past and now. I'm very curious and I belong to that group of people who use what they observe and let it come out through what they do. And I keep returning to things and people who interest me. Poor Sissy, Elizabeth, empress of Austria, I don't give her a moment's peace!' Painted by Winterhalter and bearing an uncanny resemblance in photographs to Vivien Leigh in Gone With the Wind, she is in many ways the archetype of Manolo's concept of femininity. Beautiful, high-mettled, aristocratic and gracious, she is the sort of figure from the past whom he takes and modernizes. As he says, 'Using the past can so easily be pastiche. I love the work of Winterhalter but it must be modernized if it is to have any contemporary meaning.'

Grandes dames such as the Empress of Austria hold considerable power for Manolo — and he stretches his net wide, taking in Pauline Borghese sculpted by Canova at one end of the spectrum and the Marchesa Casati at the other. What they must all have is the courage of their own style, whether flamboyant or understated, and the ability to be unselfconsciously unique.

'I love cheap movies', he claims. 'Fritz Lang…Joan Bennett. I can enjoy them all. I remember all the little things people don't normally pick up in a film. I knew the names of all the minor actors as well as the stars. I knew the directors, the cameramen, the costume designers. Movies were my absolute obsession.' And so were their stars. Manolo remembers fondly how he doodled and dressed Brigitte Bardot on all his school books when he was a teenager and how he fell in love with Gina Lollobrigida – 'so peasant'. But the star whom he admired above all others was Romy Schneider in *Il Lavoro*, 'so chic, wearing a Chanel suit and looking so worldly and sophisticated in a beautiful apartment in Milan, with Ella Fitzgerald on the record player.'

'When I arrived I was very provincial. I was from a small island, for God's sake! She formed my – how can I say? – less provincial side. It was a very necessary education. Even going with her to smart shops. There weren't any smart shops on the island. Anything smart came from across the seas. My aunt acted as a daily fashion mentor. I was so impressed by the way she carried herself. Her codes of behaviour were weird by modern standards but I believed her totally. She came from a very rich family and had lived a life of considerable privilege. Her demeanour was from another age, somehow, and she moved differently. I was still rather shy and found going to restaurants rather a strain. Once, just as we were leaving, I took her chair and pulled it out to help her rise. When we were in the car, she said, "Remember, you should never take a lady's chair too quickly. You must respect the rhythm of rising from the table."'

Thinking of modern women, he immediately pinpoints as sharing this quality with the women he admires from the past the Italian style mavin, Anna Piaggi, fashion editor of Italian *Vogue*, editor of the eighties' Italian cult magazine *Vanity* and now famed for her 'Double Pages' in *Vogue*. 'Everything she does is new', he points out. 'She is like an everyday work of art. In fact she is an artist and the tools she chooses to work with are clothes. She is the most talented and brave person in fashion. Such originality! Such intelligence! And such spontaneity! Nobody else is even remotely like her. Look, you may not always like what she does but you always have to admire the intellect behind the clothes. Nothing about her is random. The discipline: that's what's so divine about her.' It is, in his opinion, a question of originality.

This is the quality which made Tina Chow so important to him. 'She was the most important person in my life', he says simply. 'We shared the same aesthetic. Our relationship was totally symbiotic.' Her death is something from which Manolo will never fully recover. 'She played a vital part in my career. We had a total affinity in what we liked, so much so that she was the only person I would call up to talk about my shoes. We totally agreed. She was so far ahead. I don't remember anyone talking about minimalism in the seventies, but Tina was already doing it. She is the one who put a stamp on the seventies for me. She had a great influence on me but she wasn't exactly a muse: she was beyond being a muse. I'm talking of a deep kindred soul, a true friend. We would talk on the phone as many as four or five times a day. I miss her so much. If I were to sum up what made her so unique, I would say that for

me she was the most refined human being – an exquisite combination of the best of Europe and the best of the Orient.'

There have been other women whom Manolo admires and they will be looked at in later chapters but the real and lasting influence on Manolo Blahnik's creativity has been the cinema. It is the love affair of his life and it started when he was very young when Maria Socorro, his nanny, used to take him to the cinema, with his father's permission. His earliest memory is of seeing *Snow White* with her when he was four. It was love at first sight. Manolo had found the medium that would satisfy his spirit and feed his imagination more than any other. Even as a small child, he could identify with the anxiety and excitement of the maids at his family's *finca* when he heard them whispering and sighing, 'When will *Gone With the Wind* come to the island?' As he recalls, they had to wait until 1950. Like them, he felt frustrated. After all, it was the movies which most vividly brought the world to him and relieved the often tedious daily life of an island.

Blahnik remembers the cinema as a great experience but also often a frustrating one. 'The copies of the films we got were frequently badly spliced and cut. They were always breaking down. I don't know whether it was the power or what it was. Everybody would start to whistle and stamp their feet until it started again.' No matter how poor the projection, film stimulated, enlarged and illuminated Manolo's young life, feeding his imagination in a whole range of ways. He remembers: 'When I was in my teens I saw *Senso*. I almost went into a coma. I was in a state of shock. I'd never seen such a divine combination of music, costume and sets.

'Both my parents were Anglophiles and, without really being aware of it at the time, I was brought up with a strong English cultural background. We took *The Illustrated London News*, for example. I suppose my education was an informal fusion of that, Spanish and Slav. I was very lucky to be given such a wide multicultural base. And I do feel very much a product of all this.'

It was perfect!' If many sensitive teenagers tend to live in a fantasy world, Manolo Blahnik's was quite simply the world of the movies, whether masterpieces such as *Brief Encounter* or B-movies starring Barbara Stanwyck. That is why, even today, he claims, quite truthfully, to have more visual memories of the movies than any in real life. And they are often the things which anchor his thoughts, as in 'Do you remember that marvellous moment in *Come Back, Little Sheba*…?'

'I love cheap movies', he claims. 'Fritz Lang…Joan Bennett. I can enjoy them all. I remember all the little things people don't normally pick up in a film. I knew the names of all the minor actors as well as the stars. I knew the directors, the cameramen, the costume designers. Movies were my absolute obsession.' And so were their stars. Manolo remembers fondly how he doodled and dressed Brigitte Bardot on all his school books when he was a teenager and how he fell in love with Gina Lollobrigida – 'so peasant'. But the star whom he admired above all others was Romy Schneider in *Il Lavoro*, 'so chic, wearing a Chanel suit and looking so worldly and sophisticated in a beautiful apartment in Milan, with Ella Fitzgerald on the record player. And the most marvellous tuberoses. You felt you could smell them! And that pillbox hat that Jackie Kennedy took up in America. It was by Halston but its spirit was pure Chanel. These are the sort of stylistic things in films which have really put a stamp on me since I was very young.'

In fact, it was really the Italian actresses who excited him most, for their strong sexuality and rich emotional power. 'The strength of Anna Magnani', he recalls. 'I was transfixed by her face. I saw her in a restaurant in Paris once, with her son. I couldn't even look at my miserable little omelette. The power! That fifties era was the period for the best faces of the century: Mangano, Cardinale and Loren. Very southern and strong. They were beautiful but it was more than beauty. There was something so primeval about them. They were terrifying and exciting, but so desirable.'

Star-struck film fan as he was, Manolo remembers the brief, fleeting contacts he has had with the all-time screen greats – like the time outside Sotheby's when it was raining very hard. He had managed to hail a taxi and then he realized that standing next to him was Audrey Hepburn. He offered her the cab, which she accepted 'with the most devastating smile'. He is pleased that Garbo once paused outside the window of the New York store, which was decorated with croissants with shoes on top, and called in, 'They look scrumptious, don't they?'

In his lifelong involvement with the cinema, from Katharine Hepburn to Cate Blanchett, Blahnik has one all-time favourite film, based on the novel which he considers to be the greatest of the twentieth century. Luchino Visconti's version of Giuseppe Tomasi di Lampedusa's *Il Gattopardo* is, in his opinion, a flawless masterpiece to which he constantly returns, watching it in English, Italian and Spanish – he has versions in several languages. He first read the book in the fifties and claims, 'It was my great educative experience. To me it is the most extraordinary book of the century. It seemed to sum up the end of an era so perfectly, a time when the power of religion, the aristocracy and the big organic families were all breaking up and have now gone.'

Manolo recalls meeting Luchino Visconti at the Round House in London in the seventies and telling him how much he loved the film; it was an act almost of piety, so greatly does he revere the director and his work: 'He was no longer young but I could see that he had once been distinguished and glamorous in the Latin way.' Manolo goes to the cinema less now than he did but he tries to keep abreast of modern movies through videos, although he feels that contemporary films are not in the class of the great movies of the past any more than many current film stars can compete with the greats of the past.

For a man whose shoes have so often been praised for reflecting the lighthearted élan of the spirit of the rococo, it is perhaps surprising to learn that two of the greatest influences on Blahnik's

'I'm not an intellectual,' he confesses, 'but I am a voracious observer of people's movements and attitudes in the past and now. I'm very curious and I belong to that group of people who use what they observe and let it come out through what they do.'

thinking as a designer are both renowned for the monumentality of their use of material rather than its delicacy. Both have in common with Blahnik the fact that they are Spanish, but they are separated by over two centuries. They are the artist Francisco de Zurbarán – 'he makes me cry' – and the man who also admitted his indebtedness to the painter, couturier Cristobal Balenciaga who, although he has been dead for three decades, continues, along with Chanel, to exert considerable influence on many modern designers. Manolo reveres them both for their discipline with fabric, whether painted or in an actual garment. 'It's the draping that is so amazing,' he explains. 'They both had this extra-ordinarily pure, even austere, line. It was almost monastic and yet they were able to make something so beautiful. The technique is as light as a feather – in Balenciaga's case even when he's working with thick tweed.'

Manolo's favourite museum is the Prado in Madrid. He goes there as often as he can, never passing through the city without making a visit, no matter how brief it has to be in order to fit into his tight schedule. He makes straight for Velázquez and El Greco. He is less moved by Goya, although he admires his drawings: 'He has never touched me as the others do. Zurbarán's saints…in a trance…in a state of saintly convulsion, I adore it!'

In the breadth of his cultural influences, taking in film, literature and art, what makes Manolo Blahnik's appreciation different from that of most people is his critical range. He can thrill to the best, enjoy the average and even find something of interest in the bad. It is part of the exuberance and exhilaration of the man. Much of what he reads and watches is, by his own admission, trash, but a casual check of his bedside books and videos does not totally bear this out. As a man who normally only requires four or five

hours' sleep a night, he gets through many books, in English, French, Spanish and Italian, his favourites being biographies.

Piled high on either side of the bed in his Bath home, the books he was reading when I visited at the end of 1998 included Kenneth Tynan's Letters; Edmund White's biography of Jean Genet; The Ossie Clark Diaries; Gore Vidal's The Smithsonian Institute; Herbert Listz's Italian Diary; Greek Monumental Bronze Sculpture; The Baroque; Delacroix and Picasso and Photography. The piles of videos included Double Indemnity, A Place in the Sun and Possessed. Although Manolo Blahnik would be alarmed at the suggestion that he is something of a polymath, the breadth of his cultural interests sets him apart from many current designers, especially those under forty.

In fact the only designers likely to be in his league are Yves Saint Laurent and Karl Lagerfeld, both of whom are undoubtedly polymaths in the world of fashion. Like Manolo, they are of the age when they came through a particular form of academic education, one which is found less and less and is, indeed, considered less and less relevant. Whereas all three men were schooled in the idea that it is only through knowledge of the past that worthwhile things can be created in the present, current designers come with no such cultural baggage.

Blahnik has no doubt that the open, liberal approach to education taken by both his parents, who never once suggested to him or his sister what sort of career they should pursue, is what has made him the creator he is today. But he also gives credit to the time he spent in Geneva as a student under the watchful eye of his favourite relative, his father's cousin, Aunt Frederique, always known in the family as Tante Beda, who was married to the Greek ambassador to Switzerland and whose son,

Piled high on either side of the bed in the Bath home where he lives alone, the books he was reading when I visited at the end of 1998 included Kenneth Tynan's *Letters*; Edmund White's biography of Jean Genet; *The Ossie Clark Diaries*; Gore Vidal's *The Smithsonian Institute*; Herbert Listz's *Italian Diary*; *Greek Monumental Bronze Sculpture*; *The Baroque*; *Delacroix* and *Picasso and Photography*. The piles of videos included *Double Indemnity*, *A Place in the Sun* and *Possessed*. Although Manolo Blahnik would be alarmed at the suggestion that he is something of a polymath, the breadth of his cultural interests sets him apart from many current designers, especially those under forty.

Manolo's cousin George, worked with the United Nations. Frederique was, by all standards, a woman of power, stylish and rather larger than life. Manolo adored her.

Arriving in Switzerland at fifteen, he was at an impressionable age – and the person who impressed him most was his elegant aunt. Impeccably dressed, he recalls, it was the little things which made her appearance so chic, such as a Hermès bag she had in a marvellous shade of green, with everything in it – mirror, lipstick case, hairbrush – all in exactly the same matching green. She taught her nephew how to think in a sophisticated way. She drew the guidelines which a young man from a remote island had to learn in a chic international city. 'Geneva was totally divine for me', he says. 'But I suspect it was really very dull and bourgeois. Certainly life at my aunt's was both strict and formal. She was so stern but I loved it all, really.'

Manolo loved going out with his aunt to the theatre, opera and restaurants. He realizes now that it was all part of a subtle learning curve in behaviour as well as taste. 'When I arrived I was very provincial. I was from a small island, for God's sake! She formed my – how can I say? – less provincial side. It was a very necessary education. Even going with her to smart shops. There weren't any smart shops on the island. Anything smart came from across the seas. My aunt acted as a daily fashion mentor. I was so impressed by the way she carried herself. Her codes of behaviour were weird by modern standards but I believed her totally. She came from a very rich family and had lived a life of considerable privilege. Her demeanour was from another age, somehow, and she moved differently. I was still rather shy and found going to restaurants rather a strain. Once, just as we were leaving, I took her chair and pulled it out to help her rise. When we were in the car, she said, "Remember, you should never take a lady's chair too quickly. You must respect the rhythm of rising from the table." She wasn't too happy about some of my student friends. Naturally, I

was attracted to the exuberance of the Spaniards, Americans and Mexicans. They excited me because they were so crazy, so sensual. I found most Europeans boring. The kids I loved were loud. My aunt used to say, "Manolo, you must learn not to make so much noise when you speak." I learned many things from her, but not that!'

It was his father's wish that Manolo should study international law in the University of Geneva and that is the degree for which he enrolled, with more filial obedience than enthusiasm. As part of the course included medical law there came a point when the students had to visit a hospital to watch an autopsy. Manolo had been interested in medicine since his early teens, when his mother had been briefly hospitalized. He had even toyed with the idea of training to become a doctor. The morning in Switzerland when he was due to witness his first autopsy finished that idea for ever. As the cadaver was wheeled into the room, Manolo knew that he would faint if he did not get out into the fresh air immediately. He made a precipitous exit and never returned. It was not the sight of a dead body nor the thought of it being cut open that induced the overwhelming feeling of nausea. What almost overcame the young man was the smell of the formaldehyde used to preserve the corpse. The incident marked the end of any serious thoughts of a legal career, although Manolo still maintains that he found the course very interesting.

Manolo's father was sympathetic to his son's plea for a change of direction and agreed that, for the next semester, he could switch courses in order to study the arts which were so clearly much more in tune with the young man's instinctive interests. He studied international literature – predominantly English, French and Spanish – and history of art. During the summer vacations, he worked in the United Nations distributing leaflets and translating. But Geneva was beginning to bore him. He knew that he had to move on.

Page 31: From the beginning, Manolo did everything to do with publicity for his firm himself, including taking his own shots of shoes. This example of his photography is from the early seventies, when he was first beginning to make his mark as a London shoemaker.

Page 32: A Manolo Blahnik photograph of a Manolo Blahnik shoe, taken for publicity purposes in the mid-seventies.

Right: One of Manolo's favourite photographs, taken by David Seidner in Manolo's shop in Old Church Street in 1978.

OF MADNESS AND MAIDENS

'It was the best time!' he says. 'I was only at the school once in a blue moon. Are you kidding? I spent all my time at the movies. I was seeing five movies a day. Leicester Square. It was divine. London! It was so exciting, I made marvellous friends. Some of my very best and most lasting friends. I was totally ready for it.'

'It was one of those accidents of life', Manolo Blahnik claims of his becoming a shoemaker, 'I could just as well have been a milliner or a fashion designer.' In the late sixties, as he contemplated his next move after completing his studies in Geneva, neither of these paths entered his mind, although they would have been feasible possibilities even then. Lucky that parental aspirations were not brought to bear in his choice of career, Manolo nevertheless had many possibilities open to him, not least the diplomatic corps, where his social and linguistic skills would surely have been welcomed. It is pleasant to fantasize over how his extravagant personality would have shaken up that formal world of protocol, rather like De Mandeville's impact in Lawrence Durrell's *Esprit de Corps*. Certainly, the law lost a man who would have been a brilliant and mesmeric performer in court, just as the United Nations would probably have benefited from his suave ability to talk compulsively in several languages. But his growing ambition was to take his place in life along very much less conventional paths. As he now jokingly says, 'My sick little mind was aflame with ideas and possibilities.' This whirl of ideas and possibilities was acknowledgement of the intense creativity of a man who claims, 'The only two things I never actually had to be taught were how to hold a pencil and how to swim. They both came naturally, almost like a birthright.'

During his years in Geneva, Manolo had frequently visited Paris. Taking advantage of the comparative accessibility of the French capital from Switzerland, normally driving there to stay over a weekend, he and his friends went to hear the sort of concerts never staged in Switzerland: Sylvie Vartan; The Beatles, who disappointed him; Trini Lopez, who did not (Manolo can still sing 'If I Had a Hammer' right through). But even though he enjoyed his trips, Manolo was aware that Paris played second fiddle to London, still swinging, in the all-powerful and all-encompassing new wave of pop culture. London was, as they expressed it then, 'where it was at'.

Blahnik now sees as almost inevitable the fact that he moved from Geneva to Paris rather than directly to London. The whole 'swinging' aspect of the city was out of kilter with the dream of London he had nurtured since childhood. What attracted him about England was the Beatonesque world of house parties in the country, the relaxed elegance of the Duke of Windsor and, perhaps most powerfully, 'the truly, truly English country gentry, who have lived quietly and modestly – but with the highest standards and the very best understated taste – in the same house for the last six hundred years and are still wearing three-hundred-year-old tweeds, woven to last a millennium.' It was a world and a culture which had a mesmeric effect on Blahnik and still does today.

'I love the way they walk and the way they talk. Like no other nation in the world. And to me their approach to clothes is so exotic. Those marvellous large, extrovert tweeds from Savile Row! Worn by any other nation, they would look unbearably vulgar but, on the backs of the English gentry, they look nothing crude. They are just an example of that sublime English self-confidence.' Blahnik confesses that one of the earliest ways in which he

'I love the way they walk and the way they talk. Like no other nation in the world. And to me their approach to clothes is so exotic. Those marvellous large, extrovert tweeds from Savile Row! Worn by any other nation, they would look unbearably vulgar but, on the backs of the English gentry, they look nothing crude. They are just an example of that sublime English self-confidence.'

became involved with the culture of traditional English life was through his awareness of how Englishmen in the 20th century imposed their point of view through the individuality of their dress codes. As he says, 'Swinging London seemed by comparison an aberration. It was never the England that I used to dream of. Purple crushed velvet — forget it! It was all those foxy, rusty English colours that I absolutely loved.'

Manolo Blahnik left Geneva for Paris in 1965 in order to study art and, especially, to develop his skills in theatre design. In fact, although he was indeed interested in designing for the theatre — including ballet and opera — and was a fan of the work of Christian Bérard, it was still the cinema, his passion since childhood, that really fired his imagination. He was in love with the poetic quality of Cocteau's films, *L'Eternel Retour* and *L'Aigle à deux têtes*, but it was Bérard's fantastic designs for the film of *La Belle et la Bete* which thrilled him, as had *Orphée*, starring Jean Marais and Maria Casarès, with costumes by Marcel Escoffier. And, although these films were already twenty years old, there were other, more modern examples which made the idea of France and its culture exciting to the young man.

Throughout his life, Manolo Blahnik has found cultures exemplified for him by the medium of his first love and, although he was aware that Paris was not at the cutting edge of much of the world of pop culture, the cinematic history of France — like that of Italy — could not fail to enrich and deepen the experience of living in Paris. For Manolo, films were not just a seminal influence; in the hands of a great director, they were almost an educative

medium, illuminating a country and its culture for him. Just as it was through the work of Passolini, Antonioni and Fellini that Italy became familiar to him, so France was Truffaut's *Jules et Jim*, Jean Seberg and Jean-Paul Belmondo in *A bout de souffle* and the films of Jacques Demy.

Although he eventually came to see Paris as rather too bourgeois, with its arts weakened by provincial values, Manolo enjoyed his time in the city, studying art, working on his drawings of set designs and perfecting his spoken French — still, in his view, the language in which he is richest. He was very happy when he managed to get a job working in an antique shop. One of the aspects of Blahnik's character not always appreciated by those who enjoy and prefer to see only the debonair social performer — amusing and extravagantly exclamatory — is the fact that this image, not especially true in itself, is underpinned by hard work. It is possible that at any point in what must be considered Manolo's golden period of good looks, when he was in his early twenties, he could have slipped into the ranks of beautiful young men taken up by society and never asked to do anything very much apart from be attractive and entertain. But that life would have held no attraction for him. Beneath the exterior frivolities, Manolo Blahnik is a serious man who, even when young, believed in the work ethic. It is part of the deepest contradiction within him: the southern extravagance married to the northern puritanism, which comes from his particular parental mix of cultures.

Manolo spent much of his time studying with the people from L'Ecole des Beaux Arts and L'Ecole de Louvre, but he also found

Page 38: Snapped in happily extrovert mood at an Yves Saint Laurent couture show at rue Spontini, Paris, Manolo is wearing an antique coat found for him by Anna Piaggi's friend, Australian fashion historian Vern Lambert.

Left: Manolo took the photographs at the wedding of Tina and Michael Chow. This one of the bride captures the trust and intensity that characterized his relationship with Tina, making her one of his closest friends and someone with whom he communicated daily.

Right: Manolo in trademark slouch hat and Yves Saint Laurent suit, hamming it up for Barry Lategan's lens with Bianca Jagger, also wearing Yves Saint Laurent.

Page 41: Young, hip and cool, Manolo as fashionable young man in Paris – suggesting a certain English sang froid in the decorative manner of the day. In the background running is the artist Sophie Klarwein.

time to work in one of the few boutiques in Paris which was able to capture some of the contemporary quality of those in London. The job was a long way from being the most important one in Paris, but the experience it gave Manolo would prove invaluable only a few years later when he found his true trade. GO, on rue Bonaparte, was more typical of the King's Road than the Left Bank, selling clothes from the twenties and thirties, furniture and fabrics loosely called Art Nouveau and artefacts from the hippy trails. Manolo remembers it fondly: 'It was a totally mad place.... Very special, specific taste and the only place in Paris when you could buy mad, English-type things. It was very hip and very young. Owned by two divine women, Giselle Menhenett and Odile Wood.'

Saint-Germain-des-Prés was the 'swinging' area of Paris, thronged with students, bohemians and actors. With luck, you might bump into Françoise Hardy or Françoise Dorleac. If you were very lucky you might find yourself face to face with Catherine Deneuve or even Bardot. But not everyone came to the Left Bank looking for stars. The process was reversed in the case of

Manolo. Many young Parisians, including stars, came to look at him. He was famous at GO for his good looks and extreme behaviour. And he had his groupies, not least Anouk Aimée, who used to bring her daughter to GO – both were much more interested in watching Manolo than in trying on the clothes.

It was at this time that Manolo met Paloma Picasso, who was living in Paris. Her illustrious name and her work as a jewellery designer meant that she knew virtually all the artistic and creative people in Paris. She and Manolo got on immediately, soon becoming very close friends, as they have remained for the rest of their lives. As he claims, 'We're so close she is family, really. I owe so much to Paloma for the help she gave me in the early days, introducing me to people in Paris and New York. We had such fun when we were young. I adore her dramatic Latin taste. I've been so lucky to be able to be near such an amazing woman.'

Manolo frequently popped over to London and, in agreement with his father, decided that it was time to cross the Channel permanently. Not only were his social and artistic needs more likely to be catered for in London than in Paris; it was time for him to

perfect his English. He enrolled in the Davies School of English, in Queensway. He remembers it warmly. 'It was the best time!' he says. 'I was only at the school once in a blue moon. Are you kidding? I spent all my time at the movies. I was seeing five movies a day. Leicester Square. It was divine. London! It was so exciting, I made marvellous friends. Some of my very best and most lasting friends. I was totally ready for it.'

Blahnik had chosen the perfect time to arrive. London in the seventies was to be a very different place from the city of the sixties. It began to broaden its spectrum and to settle down. The axis of youth and fashion, having fluctuated between Carnaby Street in the West End and King's Road in Chelsea, swung permanently to Fulham and Chelsea, which took the lead as the fashionable heart of young London, a role the area has kept for more than twenty years.

On the back of the vibrant pop music industry – largely fuelled by working-class talent – Carnaby Street had always been a fashion mecca for East End, suburban and even provincial lads who wanted their gear to have the authenticity of their class.

Young public schoolboys were briefly seduced into following them until Mr Fish and Blades made sharp dressing as much a prerogative of the privileged as of the social underdog. Fashion became an obsession for the upper as well as the middle classes as high society, piqued at missing out on the fun, subsumed what it considered good for its own world – led by the first style magazines, which had become the new taste makers of the post-swinging-London generation.

By the beginning of the seventies, society had recaptured the fashionable life. Mara and Lorenzo Berni opened San Lorenzo. Kasmin was one of the most controversial avant-garde art dealers in London. John Stefanidis, the Greek-born interior decorator, was busy, along with David Hicks, creating beautiful homes for the rich. Socialite Nicky Waymouth held open house in her Chelsea home, once the studio of Augustus John. Ossie Clark dominated fashion just as his friend David Hockney towered over the art world. The world of London fashion was ruled by the best editors of fashion and society magazines England has ever produced. Willie Landels, Viennese exile from World War II, made *Harper's & Queen* the

Above: An early advertising picture
of stylist Florence Nicaise taken by
Manolo Blahnik. So at home was
Blahnik behind the camera, and
so talented at capturing his
own vision, that a career as a
photographer remained a distinct
and attractive possibility. It seems
distinctly improbable now, but
Manolo's earliest appearances in
Vogue were as a photographer
rather than a shoemaker.

mouthpiece of the Chelsea set, just as Beatrix Miller made *Vogue* into the world leader in the Condé Nast stable – quixotic, even fey, but always quintessentially English in its tastes and moods.

It was rich soil for the elegant, handsome and capricious Manolo. With his chocolate-soldier manners and operatic behaviour – part *Der Rosenkavalier*, part *Die Fledermaus* – he might have been especially crafted for the new London, glittering around Chelsea. He wanted to stay, but to do that he needed a work permit. His guardian angel came from Paris. Giselle Menhenett suggested he meet Joan Burstein, at that time proprietor of a highly successful boutique in Kensington called Feathers. They understood each other's worth instantly and Burstein gave Manolo a job, initially looking after sales of New Man jeans at Feathers. 'I was always tidying the shelves and making stock lists. It could have been boring but I was also helping to look after the press. We had endless phone calls: "Do you have any Cacharel jumpers?" "We need a dress by Emmanuelle Khanh." I learned so much about the actual business of fashion retailing. But above all, I learned so much from Mrs Burstein, a divine woman who had the most brilliantly sharp fashion eye.'

It was whilst he was at Feathers that Manolo met the man who was to become one of his closest friends. Eric Boman was waiting for a bus in Kensington High Street when he became aware that everybody in the queue was watching a thin young man crossing the road in the face of heavy traffic, holding up his hand to stop it as he crossed. 'He had a bushy, golliwog hairdo', he recalls, 'and he was wearing a very long cardigan. He had come out of Feathers because he'd seen me and wanted to catch me before the bus came. I was wearing a very small leather jacket and the sleeves had been lengthened by knitting. I had on cowboy boots and brown cord jeans.'

Manolo had already begun to make lots of fashion contacts on a good level, not only through his social life but also through Feathers which, as one of London's most trusted avant-garde shops, was visited by top journalists from all the magazines and newspapers. He had been asked casually by a friend on *Vogue*, Catharine Milinaire, to find subjects for a possible feature on people in London who dressed in an extraordinary way. With his usual zeal, if he spotted someone he rushed to make contact, even if he had never seen the person before.

Eric Boman recalls that he was invited to a party at Manolo Blahnik's flat in Warwick Square, which he was sharing with Catharine Milinaire's brother, Gilles. 'I walked all the way to Belgravia from Battersea, where I was living at the time. There wasn't a soul there, nor was there any furniture. It was the most beautiful, big elegant space, with marvellous floorboards. There were incense sticks stuck between them. We sat in the kitchen. Manolo asked me if I were hungry, adding, "I have jam and sugar – and maybe some condensed milk". There was a long shelf running along one wall and on it was every sort of Tiptree jam. Manolo opened a Tate and Lyle bag of sugar and, dipping in a soup spoon, ate vast quantities.'

Manolo Blahnik was, as now, hyperactive, ablaze with nervous energy. He needed quick energy fixes and obtained them by existing almost entirely on a sugar diet. As he says himself, he had no interest in food. He was reluctant to take the time required to sit and eat a meal, unless the company and conversation were very good, and was certainly not interested in cooking for himself. However, as they became friends, Boman recalls that when he cooked such dishes as lentil and ham-hock soup, Manolo adored them and ate heartily. 'We both had bourgeois taste in food', he recalls. 'Even at a place like San Lorenzo Manolo always had the

Right: An advertising shot taken by Manolo of which he has remarked with commendable understatement: 'I was possessed by bows at that time'. Presentation has always been of the utmost importance in selling Blahnik shoes. Here, the tied ends of the cushion make it resemble some piece of delicious confectionery.

veal so overcooked it was totally dry, with no goodness whatever left in it.'

One of Blahnik's other friends at this time was a set decorator called Peter Young, who worked in films and was a friend of the actress Coral Browne. He encouraged Manolo in his designing ambitions and was the first person to open up the possibility of his designing shoes. Young had a friend who worked for a tiny shop in Chelsea called Zapata. Young and Manolo decorated the shop in a post-sixties funky style, with yellow walls, faux-naïf cows, trees and clouds and fake grass on the floor. Manolo had already begun to employ his set-designing skills by making decorations for children's parties, and he found the spirit of Zapata and its decoration in character with the giant cut-out fruit, flowers and toadstools he was creating.

Blahnik found party decorating amusing but it could never be a full-time job, any more than it could occupy and satisfy his creative intensity. At this stage, he was flaying around in a creative dervish dance as he looked for the field that would accommodate his skills, aspirations, ambitions and, above all, his temperament. Febrile, restless, discontented and desperately searching on one side, exuberant, witty, imaginative and original on the other, Manolo Blahnik needed a serious occupation to channel his enormous creative urge. He had already become a personality in London's social world, courted for his good looks, his international sophistication and his extraordinarily original personality, which was a result of a hypersensitive, naturally extrovert character – and a great deal of play-acting. Manolo has always known the the-

atrical skills of timing and movement. No man outside the acting profession knows better how to command the space around him and rivet attention on what he is saying.

As a young man, Blahnik's torrents of words were famous. Out it all poured, in no special order and rarely in one language: insights, prejudices, overstatements, extreme sophistication. No wonder London fell at his feet. Eric Boman points out, 'He was much more eccentric in those days. He's calmed down a lot over the years. I think he was striving for recognition and it's that recognition – on a world scale – that has calmed him. When we were young he was permanently over the top and theatrical, totally dedicated to shocking people. A true Latin, he would scream with enthusiasm at people in the street, so excited was he about their appearance. He couldn't help drawing attention to himself. His craziness often totally exhausted me. He never stopped talking. But after Sweden, where I was born, the warmth and passion of his convictions were marvellous for me. I'm so grateful to have known him – and I'm sure that goes for everybody else at that time.'

In 1971, Eric Boman, Paloma Picasso and Manolo went to New York (see Chapter 4). When he returned to London, Manolo had made his great career decision after several years of experimenting. He would become a shoemaker. Boman says the decision was the end of a process he had been observing for some time. 'Manolo was looking for a focus,' he points out. 'He had been a little bit lost for some time. He was looking for something that would present a challenge, exercise to the full his huge creative

Manolo Blahnik

Spring and summer 1976 — Style Piaggi

Black and white kid skin

potential — and make him happy. He was smart enough to know that if he wanted success on all levels of life he would have to specialize, so that's what he did.' Blahnik became design consultant at the company behind Zapata and the first shoes he designed were not for women but for men. Even at this early stage in his career, making shoes was already a hands-on business for Manolo. He created a range of saddle shoes, to be made in Northampton, the centre of British shoe manufacture, and he went to the factory, not only to learn about the craft but to make sure the shoes were made properly.

One of Manolo's friends at this time was Peter Schlesinger, who was a close friend of David Hockney. The painter loved the colours of Manolo's co-respondent shoes. They had chalk white crepe soles made in Northampton and electric blue and vivid lime uppers. Although Hockney and Manolo's friends wore them, they were not a commercial success. Even if they had been, he would not have found men's footwear a sufficiently taxing or varied field for his imagination. As he says, 'Men's shoes are very limited. I mean, what can you do with a proper English brogue? I

love Clark's and all those classic English shoes, so many of which have disappeared now. They can't really be improved upon without introducing the sort of fashion element I really don't like in men's clothing. Anything too fashionable always makes me uncomfortable.' That being said, Blahnik is a fastidious dresser whose name frequently appears on the world's best-dressed lists. When he was young, he had his suits made by Tommy Nutter but, for many years now, has had classic suits made for him by Anderson and Sheppard in Savile Row — not always in classic fabrics and usually with little dandy touches such as turned-back cuffs on the sleeves. Even in the early seventies, the young man was known for the individuality of his dress.

It was only a few months after the debut of his men's range that Blahnik's great break came. Through a friend, Chelita Secunda, he had met Ossie Clark, with whom she worked, at that time the flamboyant leader of a London school of fashion. Manolo was also encouraged at this time by Beatrix Miller, editor of *Vogue*, and her brilliant stylist, ex-model Grace Coddington who featured young English designers regularly in the magazine. Pablo and Delia, Jean

Muir and Bill Gibb were the shining stars in this galaxy but Clark was the only one with a truly international profile. Manolo was delighted to be given the commission to create the shoes for his spring-summer 1972 collection.

The shoes were almost a disaster, as might be expected when it is recalled that Manolo Blahnik is entirely self-taught, never having studied shoemaking in a college nor taken an apprenticeship in order to learn the trade. It was that very lack of training, however, that gave him the edge of originality over other London shoemakers, from the established, such as Edward Rayne, holder of the royal warrant, to the commercial, such as Ravel, Kurt Geiger, Sacha and Charles Jourdan, to the highly fashionable – in particular, Richard Smith of Chelsea Cobbler, whose name runs neck-and-neck with Manolo Blahnik at Zapata in the credits of *Vogue* for much of the seventies.

It was to be expected that the man described by *Woman's Wear Daily* in 1973 as 'one of the most exotic spirits in London' would create shoes which were, if not wearable, then certainly newsworthy. As *Vogue* itself said in the year of his debut, 'If you're buying shoes, employ a sense of humour.' The problem with the shoes that Blahnik provided for Ossie Clark was a basic design one, in a practical rather than aesthetic sense. His collection consisted of ten models, including a green sandal with a seven-inch heel of rubber. He knew nothing about tensile strengths and, in the words of Joan Juliet Buck, current editor of French *Vogue*, 'Yes, it bent. Not always, not at first, but eventually.' It could have been the disastrous end of a career nipped in the bud, but the shoes were so much fun that the fashion world forgave. Manolo began to have his shoes made in Turners, a factory in Leytonstone, east London, where old hands had the skills and experience to know what could and could not actually be made, let alone worn without danger.

It was the beginning of a career which took off remarkably quickly. By July 1973 the prestigious US trade journal *Footwear News* ran a picture of Blahnik high heels on the front page. Under the headline 'Shaft', the copy read, 'This is the most talked-about shoe in London.' It was exactly the right accolade, from the right source, at the right moment.

DRAWINGS

Glossy pink patent   leather

Manolo Blahnik London 1971 —

The 'bougie' - the metal-wedge

Manolo Blahnik. winter 1978-77

Manolo Blahnik 76-77

Manol. Blahnik - 1986 - style

"Orientelie" ... ...

Pink baroque pearls and semi-
precious stones created for Rome Picollo - 86 - ...

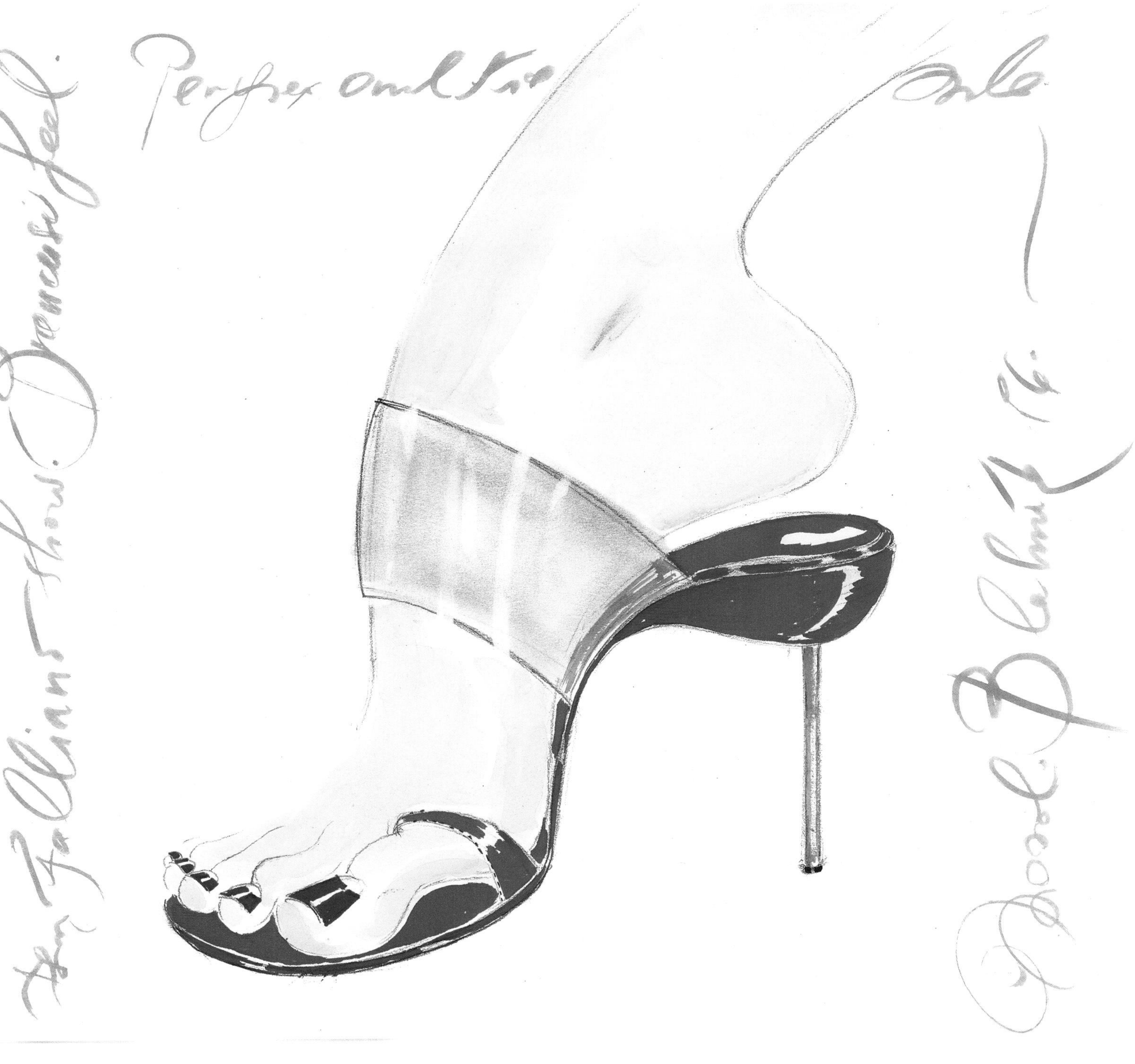

Blahník Inner 1994 Cord in sterling silver

Aluminium proper sole steel heel

The "Bandage"-wrap around the leg and in elastic raphia

Summer 1997. Paul Blondin.

Jimmy Choo

Donald Blackwell Summer 1999 Sandra

Manolo Blahnik — 1986 —

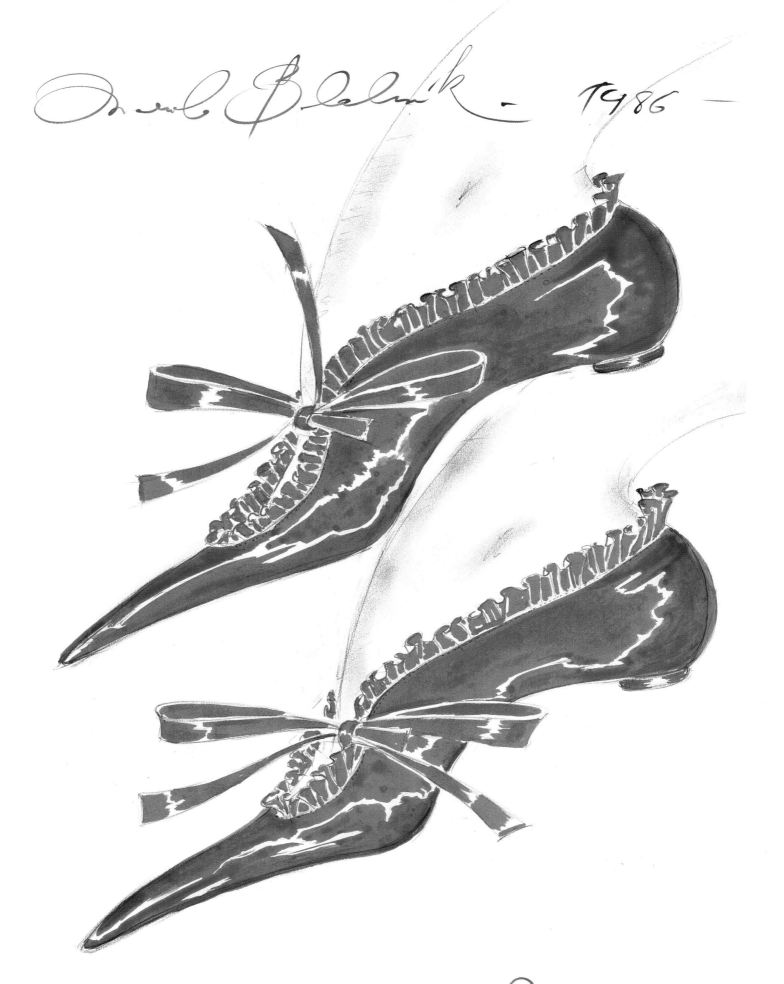

Style "Prada" Winter 86-87. London

sty.c. Elizabeth of Austria. Repal. 94 version

*wider 1999-2000 Manolo Blahnik —
made in "silver" terciopel. de seda. fringed
in emeralds. and beads.*

Style: "Monianta"
wool embroidered silk. "Foster Trilly" in relief

Winter 1999 - 2000, Manolo Blahnik

Style : Tigra : Hannibal ottoman - goat black "hair"
lining : "Leopardino"

Mule. Autumn ~ Winter 1999 ~ 2000 . London .

Manolo Blahnik

Styli Dravinfions
Mules for winter 1999-2000.

Dyed Sable and goatskin with silk linings. Manolo Blahnik

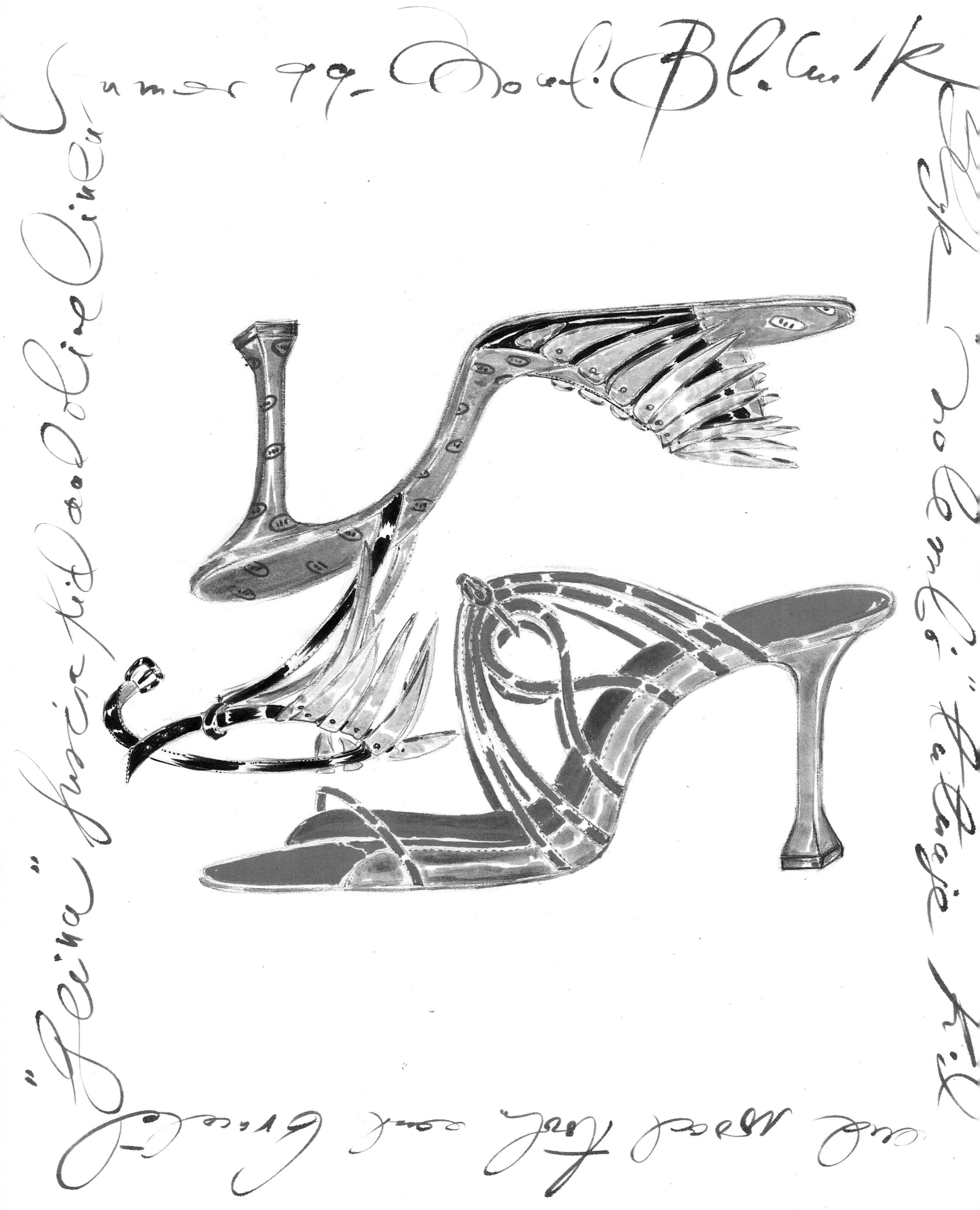
Summer 99 - Manolo Blahnik

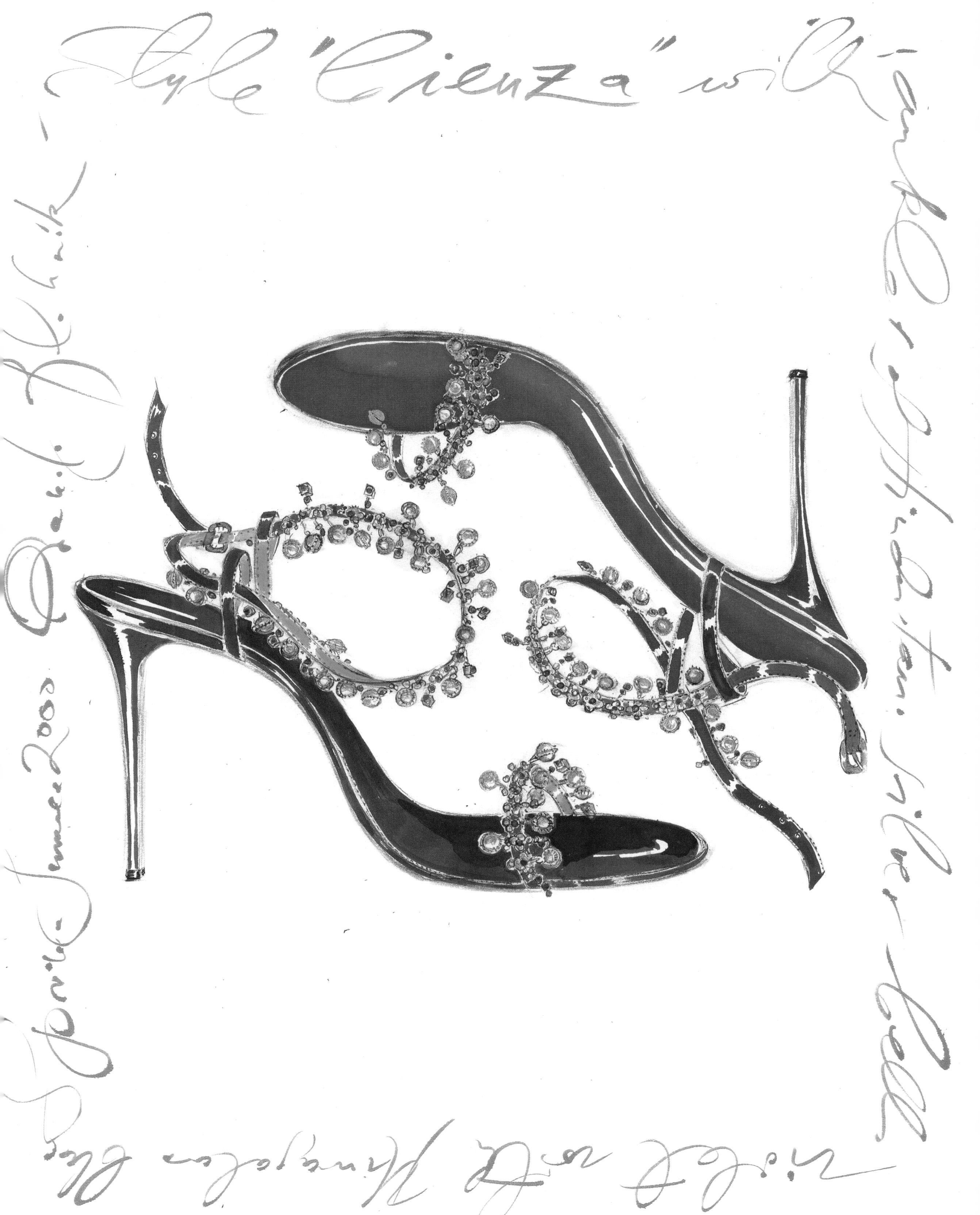
Spring Summer 2000

Style: Mariastella – Dolce Ottoman Caserta
Strass chain – Buckle colori lenticchia silver thread.

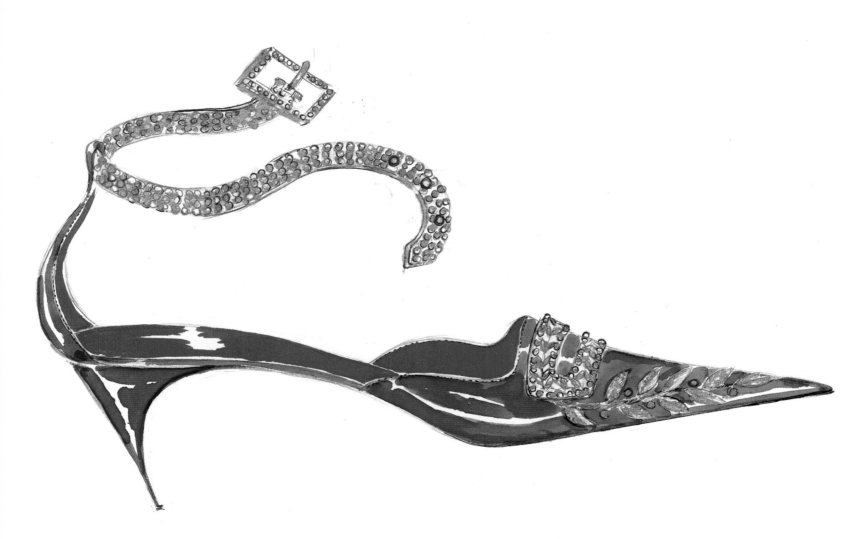

Winter 1999 – 2000. The Queen of Naples Collection
Manolo Blahnik. Ottoman silk.

Manolo Blahnik

The "Lorca" satin shoe. Granada
carnation "claveles" petals and pois
embroidered in 3.D. Winter 99-2000

BRAVE NEW WORLD

Whilst work on the Barneys New York store on Madison was being completed, the building work was screened by this photograph by Steven Meisel, styled by Ronnie Cooke Newhouse, of Linda Evangelista holding the ultimate high-fashion symbol for sophisticates – a 'Manolo'.

Little hand on the nine. Big hand on the twelve.

BARNEYS NEW YORK

Manolo Blahnik's relationship with America and its culture began when he was very young and used to wait eagerly for his mother's copy of US *Vogue* to arrive at their home in the Canary Islands. From its pages, he subconsciously drew attitudes not only toward fashion but also to society and the arts.

Manolo Blahnik's relationship with America and its culture began when he was very young and used to wait eagerly for his mother's copy of US *Vogue* to arrive at their home in the Canary Islands. From its pages, he subconsciously drew attitudes not only toward fashion but also to society and the arts. In the fifties, the very best fashion magazines – of which US *Vogue* was perhaps the supreme example – assumed certain attitudes and attributes in their readers which can no longer be taken for granted today.

In a sense, what were called 'the glossies' were as much social primers as recorders of fashion. The woman who read *Vogue* did not simply learn how to dress with style and taste. She learned how her table should be set, her flowers arranged and her menu chosen. But she learned more. The magazine's famous 'People Are Talking About…' pages were a checklist of what was happening in the arts: which painter was exhibiting where, what novels were being published, the play to see, the opera to know about. They were supplemented by articles by major figures in the arts who were sometimes given a brief to simplify complex social, historical or even philosophical arguments for the reader, or sometimes expected to amuse and entertain in a lighthearted way, even if, in their own field, they were heavy hitters. Occasionally, even scientists and politicians appeared within the covers of *Vogue*.

For a young boy like Manolo, butterfly-brained and endlessly curious, the pages of *Vogue* were an essential monthly stimulus that helped him to fall in love with the elegance and sophistication of the rarefied lives of the rich, whether in Manhattan or the Blue Grass country, Bal Harbor or San Francisco. In case the diet were too exotic, Manolo could come back down to earth by seeing the other sides of America, often reflected with harrowing truth to detail in the movies that Hollywood was still churning out with great conviction, even if the golden age of American film was passing. As he had since childhood, Manolo went to the cinema as often as he could and drank in whatever the moviemakers cared to offer their audience. Lana Turner, Greer Garson, Bette Davis: the stars taught Manolo the ways not only of women in general – their speech, demeanour, dress and deportment – but of American women in particular.

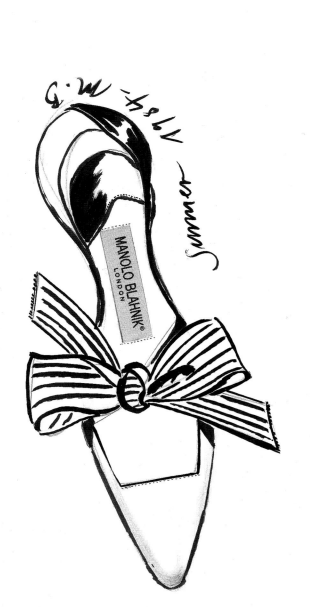

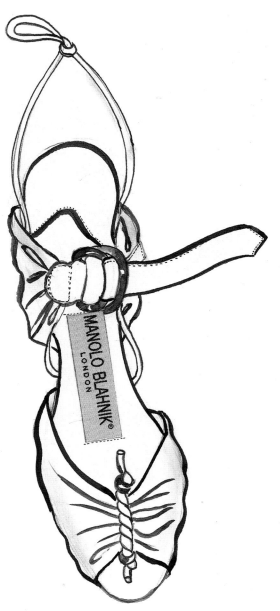

Manolo learned very much more, using the movies as his searchlight on the ways of big cities – New York, Chicago and Los Angeles – or small-town life as lived in the Midwest in states so vast as to defy the imagination of an island boy, or the decent middle-class lives of the entire North American continent. *All About Eve*, *Sunset Boulevard*, *East of Eden*, *The Big Sleep*, *A Star is Born*: the breadth of the American movies of the fifties and early sixties meant that a dedicated filmgoer like Manolo Blahnik knew a considerable amount about the mores of American life even though he had never visited the country. Add to this a range of reading that took in John Steinbeck, Ernest Hemingway, Eudora Welty and Dorothy Parker and it is apparent that the young man who first visited the United States in 1969 did so not as an innocent but as a person with certain expectations. The visit came about in Manolo's madcap period, when he was eagerly stretching out his hand to all experiences, no matter how unlikely, and ready to take any opportunity, regardless of how unpromising. The United States could not fail to be an awfully big adventure for Manolo Blahnik.

Manolo has always responded wholeheartedly and enthusiastically to friends, ready to give them the benefit of the doubt and, perhaps more important, prepared to quell his own doubts until they have been overturned or confirmed by experience. Eternally bright-eyed and eager, Manolo as a young man was, to use a modern expression, up for anything, so long as it was not illegal and held the possibility of being new, different and exciting.

Shortly after he arrived in London from Paris, Manolo met two Ukrainian sisters who were proteges of Zandra Rhodes, at that time a rising fashion star already noted for the originality of her approach and the singlemindedness of her vision. Easily impressed when a young man, Manolo became excited when Oxanna and Miroslava discussed with him their plan to go to America to take advantage of the fact that 'swinging' London was well ahead of New York in fashion design and would enjoy the kudos home-produced designers lacked. The sisters suggested that they should all three go to Washington, where they had contacts, have clothes made there, then take them to New York to sell them in the boutiques and 'little' shops which had opened as a result of the

Tied and true: Blahnik's blue-suede shoe, with the "fuerte" heel.

Manolo Blahnik, New York.

Leopard-skin high-heels made for the Gloria Vanderbilt collection in 1983 – Manolo Blahnik

excitement that had swept out from Carnaby Street and the King's Road. America, like most of the rest of the world, was eager to be part of the swinging scene.

To a keen young man it must have seemed a seductive scenario, especially when the three agreed that he would design the clothes. So he went. Looking back now, Manolo can see that it was a doomed enterprise. 'They were totally mad people', he says, 'although they were great fun to be with.' Living in a room for $5 per week, designing banal twin-sets, tops and simple dresses, working in a basement and taking the clothes to Latina, their main outlet in America, soon began to dampen the excitement and Manolo returned to London. 'I learned a bit', he admits. 'But I knew that end of the fashion world, and even designing clothes, was not really for me. I wasn't so much in love with America and I missed London.' He laughs: 'I still remember those horrific *panne de velour* dresses we used to cut out and sew in that basement!'

It was to be another two years before Blahnik would return to America and the second visit was of a very different kind. This time he went not to work but to make contacts, not to

Washington but to New York – and he went with his closest friends, Eric Boman and Paloma Picasso. Paloma, who was then designing furs for a French company, was already in New York when the two men arrived. She knew Andy Warhol and was a regular visitor to the Factory. In fact, Manolo had met many of its habitués in London so it was not surprising that, the pair having landed in New York with nowhere to stay, Paloma should take them to the Factory. Boman recalls his shock when the door was opened by Joe Dallesandro, already a world name from his roles in Warhol's films, who was busily sweeping the floor. 'I nearly fainted,' he says. 'There he was. The most beautiful creature in the world. Then we saw Paul Morrissey, who we had met in London. He knew of an apartment which was free on 19th Street and 3rd, I think – and so we moved in.'

That night, they were invited to a party for the birthday of Richard Berstein, who designed the covers of Warhol's magazine, *Interview*. It was, Boman recalls, the perfect Blahnik party: 'Everybody you needed to know was at that party.' It was the beginning of a marvellous holiday, but a holiday with intent. Both

The window of the Manolo Blahnik New York store, photographed by Pamela Hanson in December 1998. The shoe stands were made in England by Christopher Baker.

Left: A line of elegant Manolos photographed by Marc Hispard in the colourful surroundings of St Barts in the Caribbean for the December 1991 edition of US Vogue.

Right: Brilliantly coloured Manolo sandals for summer 1999, photographed by Carlyne Cerf de Dudzeele for the American edition of Marie Claire.

Plucked off another island, Capri: thong mules that are as suited for the beach as they are for dancing. By Manolo Blahnik about $385 a pair. Bergdorf Goodman; Manolo Blahnik, NYC; Neiman Marcus. Details, more stores, see In This Issue.

265

men had brought samples of their work to show prospective employers, although they were not too sure who they might be. Paloma Picasso was invaluable. 'She knew everybody', Boman says, 'And her name was like a key to New York. Use it and you were given an appointment. It opened all doors.'

One of the most important was the door marked 'Mrs Vreeland' at Condé Nast. Paloma and her friend, photographer Maurice Hogenboom, took Manolo to meet the famous editorial director of *Vogue* but, according to Boman, it was just after she had been surreptitiously removed from that role and moved out of the famous red office she had created for herself in order to make room for the new incumbent, Grace Mirabella. As a sop, her new office had been painted Vreeland red but lacked the 'big cat' carpeting and rattan furniture of the *Vogue* office. It had no equivalent of the famous pinboard that had been covered with Vreeland's unique selection of photographs and tearsheets of things she found stimulating.

Mrs Vreeland saw Manolo alone. 'I was terrified', he says. 'I was so frightened I could hardly speak. I felt like a little peasant cobbler showing his wares to a grand dame. Mrs Vreeland was charming. I remember, she kept making appreciative cooing noises as she looked at my drawings, which were mainly for sets and costumes with various other things, including drawings of shoes, thrown in. I was wearing a red-and-white cotton gingham suit.

Can you imagine? Like a walking tablecloth. She must have thought I was mad. I could barely walk because I was wearing tiny Victorian shoes, far too small, which were killing me. And there was the woman I'd idolized, in front of me. No wonder I was too frightened to speak.'

But he could listen and what Diana Vreeland was saying was of great importance. 'Hmm', she said, tilting back her head and looking long and hard at the shoe drawings. 'These things are grand…hmmm…very nice.' She turned over a few more pages and stopped, again at his drawings of shoes. 'How amazing', she said. Then, energized, she looked up and said, 'Young man, do things. Do accessories. Do shoes.' Manolo was dismissed, delirious with excitement but not so delirious that he threw caution to the winds. He sought a second opinion, going to China Machado at *Harper's Bazaar* for her verdict. It was much the same as Vreeland's. Arrangements were made for a meeting with Jerry Miller, an executive at Bendel's, the prestigious fashion store. He was enthusiastic and suggested that Manolo leave his drawings, saying, 'We're going to think seriously about this. We'll send them to the factory.' Like a little lamb, Manolo gave him all the ideas he'd drawn. He never heard from Jerry Miller again.

But he had made a great ally in Diana Vreeland and, until her death in 1989, he never failed to visit her whenever he went to New York, often with his friend André Leon Talley, who was very

Left: Like fish in a net, caught at high tide, these archetypal Manolo Blahniks were photographed for US Vogue by Oberto Gili in 1991. Manolo's frequent use of brilliant colour owes much to the sunshine and quality of light of his childhood home in the Canary Islands.

Right: A fashion shoot styled by Polly Mellen for US Vogue featuring shoes by Blahnik, photographed by Walter Chin.

was a great success, with customers queuing to make multiple purchases. It was an important step toward creating a higher North American profile, although Manolo already had a loyal following in Bloomingdales, where he had launched an exclusive range for the store the previous year. The Bloomingdales range included a classic Blahnik design, timeless and simple: a flat pump with the leather of the upper casually knotted but otherwise devoid of any design or decorative additions.

Things did not go well with Blahnik's North American collaborators, however. His fashion profile was riding high, thanks to the coverage his shoes received in the fashion magazines and a brief retrospective exhibition of his shoes, held in the Droll/Kolbert gallery in Manhattan, to highlight his most noteworthy designs from the last five years, but the designer began to realize that he was working with the wrong people. Anxious not to lose the ground he had captured in New York, he began to look for a practical solution to a problem that was beginning to make him hate America in general and American business partners in particular. The solution came at a tangent, through Dawn Mello, at

that time an executive vice-president of Bergdorf Goodman, who had on her staff a talented young copywriter in the ads department called George Malkemus. Knowing of his interest in shoes and well aware of Blahnik's dissatisfaction with things as they stood in Madison Avenue, she suggested a meeting.

Although George Malkemus and his business partner, Anthony Yurgaitis, were enthusiastic enough to fly to London for a meeting with Blahnik, the designer himself was extremely cautious, determined not to find himself again working with someone incapable of appreciating his beliefs. Nevertheless he was sufficiently interested to ask his friend André Leon Talley to meet Malkemus in New York and report back. The report was favourable and the negotiations took a more serious turn, although still not without reservations and even suspicions on Manolo's part. Malkemus recalls, 'We had meetings, meetings and more meetings.' The resolution came quite suddenly from an unexpected source. Manolo discovered that the other men shared his love of dogs, particularly Westies and Scotties. Reassured, he finally decided to sign the contract.

special effects
about this season's
dramatics. All the
are enriched with

Nothing shy
accessories: they're going in for big-time
add-ons – from boots to gloves –
bold, nearly Byzantine ornamentation

*Left: An André Leon Talley shoot
for US Vogue by Pascal Chevallier,
featuring a chair made for Marie-
Helène and Guy de Rothschild.
Taken on location at their home,
Château Ferrières, France.*

*Right: Elegance in a pair of blue
jeans: shoes from the 1999
summer collection, photographed
by Raymond Meier for British
Vogue.*

In effect, the deal enabled Malkemus and Yurgaitis to buy back from Blahnik's previous partners the licensing agreement for North and South America and to open a new shop in his name; they would also negotiate agreements with selected stores, such as Barneys, Bergdorf Goodman and Neiman Marcus, to sell Blahnik shoes. It was a perfect solution for a man who knew that he had to expand but was cautious about doing so. Manolo needed strong business partners to enable growth on his terms.

They began working with Blahnik in 1982. In 1984, *USA Today* was predicting that the New York shop would do a million dollars' worth of trade before the end of the year. Malkemus explained exactly why: 'Manolo is no longer a hard-to-find, word-of-mouth show designer. His shoes are already starting to enjoy a big success around the country.' It was the beginning of the retail miracle that would reach fever point by the mid-nineties, with women buying as many as fifty pairs of shoes at a time in the New York and London boutiques.

Manolo gives total credit for the upsurge in his fortunes to George Malkemus's brilliant entrepreneurial skills, but he himself

had reached the right point in his career to enable it to take off with wise guidance. For that Manolo gives credit to the years he had already worked with American designers. 'It was marvellous working with Calvin Klein', he recalls. 'So liberating. He'd say something very simple, like "think Chanel", and then would leave it to my imagination. The Americans are so professional. In a sense, the whole big business thing there wasn't really me but I enjoyed the experience. The people were incredible. I also adored working at Ann Klein. That was also a wonderful experience because of the divine people I worked with. Working there was a real challenge. I was involved with seven different manufacturers. It really enlarged my horizons. I not only learned about how the American system works, I also learned how important the politics of work are in America.'

If Blahnik appreciates what Malkemus has done for his business, the American feels he is much the more indebted of the two. 'He's so full of electricity and enthusiasm', he claims. 'He's like an effervescent bottle of water choked at the neck; it can explode or just fizzle out at the sides. The marvellous thing about Manolo is

he never just fizzles out. He's an ignited, volatile person but can take that spark and calm it down – and then he's at his creative peak. The energy level is formidable. He's always challenging himself but that's the vulnerable side of him coming out.' It is a challenge he faces strongly. Expansion in the Far East with a new partner, Larry Fong, has already begun, with two shops in Hong Kong and various outlets around the Pacific Rim.

But the major challenge facing Manolo Blahnik is simply the amount of work he has to pack into any year. He produces two major collections but also adds to them specifically for the American market. 'A resort collection, an evening collection – these middle collections are very important for America,' Malkemus explains. 'People travel much more in America than in Europe. They go to the sun and they want something new to wear when they get there. Basically, the London and New York shops are synchronized when it comes to selling the main collections but we have such a big wholesale business in America. Now that stores want their shoes earlier, they are always ahead in places like Neiman's and Bergdorf's.' Blahnik now has four Neiman's outlets, in Houston, Chicago, San Francisco and the biggest boutique, in Los Angeles.

It is to these boutiques that Manolo travels twice a year on his 'Meet Manolo Blahnik' promotional tours, probably the most spectacular of the innovations introduced by George Malkemus. Initially, Manolo had reservations. He wished to preserve his pose as the hard-working artisan behind the scenes and was not convinced that meeting his customers en masse would be either good public relations or creatively rewarding. He admits also that he was a little scared because, although an extravagant, extrovert social performer, he was used to a specific, highly sophisticated audience of fashion followers. How would the great American public react to his theatricality and verbal flair? How many outside the narrow confines of the insider fashion world would understand the references to artists, writers, couturiers and so on with which he sprinkles his conversation?

It is a token of the respect and affection in which Manolo Blahnik holds George Malkemus that he agreed to give it a try. The results were successful beyond all of Malkemus's dreams, not only increasing sales dramatically but, even more important for the future, raising Blahnik's personal profile across the United States. Both men work very hard on these promotional tours. Malkemus arranges every detail, including the all-important

ANTEBELLUM GARDENER

Artfully arrayed in Gerald O'Hara's hand-me-downs, sole man Manolo Blahnik is Tara's gardener (as well as pump-and-slipper consultant). Backdrop painted by French set designer Stéfan Lubrina.

appearances on television – as many as seven chat shows a day. Manolo himself stresses the importance of touring colleges, which enables him to keep in touch with the creativity and spirit of the next generation of Americans, the young women who will keep his name going on.

Women flock to meet Blahnik and occasions that start decorously soon give way to the hysteria just beneath the surface as the shoemaker is treated with all the reverence and excitement that used to greet silent movie stars. In many respects the adulation he is subject to on these occasions is exactly parallel to the fan worship that surrounded Hollywood icons of the past.

Blahnik dismisses such parallels as absurd but those who have observed his personal appearances in stores do not think the comparison so far-fetched. Just as the movie star Valentino was the focus for the sexual fantasies of women, so Blahnik, the creator of the sexiest shoes in the world, is the focus, if not of their longing, then certainly of their gratitude. They show it in a way that Malkemus as a businessman finds most gratifying. They buy. In quantity. As *The Houston Chronicle* described it in June 1999, these are fast-moving occasions, driven by a collective fear of being left behind. 'At 10:00 A.M.,' it reported, 'the couture salon at Neiman Marcus Galleria was stocked to overflowing with Manolos. By noon, it was a disaster scene. The occasion was a party in honor of the shoe wizard Manolo Blahnik, whose often way-out and teetering high-heeled sandals send women over the edge with desire – and they came on this morning to meet the designer and have him autograph their favourites. They toast him with wine, champagne and shoe-shaped cookies.'

Caught up in the hysteria of the occasion, no woman normally expects to leave the presentation without having bought at least two pairs of shoes. Many buy considerably more. Most ask Blahnik to sign the shoes on the instep. Often they buy two pairs of the same shoe, intending one for wear and the other to be treated as a quasi-religious work of art or a reliquary of an experience of mystical power. Legends abound. The press claim that many women display their Manolos on the mantlepiece of their elegant drawing rooms. Others are said to have them in glass cases on the walls, lit by directional spotlights. One journalist suggested that the perfect place for such entrancing shoes was at the foot of the bed so that the eyes, new-opened with morning, could alight on objects of beauty that would colour attitudes to the day ahead.

As an intelligent man, Manolo dismisses such extravagances; as a smart man, he does not do so loudly. He knows that the fantasy is an essential prop in the Manolo Blahnik mystique. He is aware that, tacitly at least, he must go along with the hyperbole if these appearances are to continue to break sales records with each new season. He understands that this is the nature of American retail culture. Blahnik is aware that, whereas in other parts of the world women are content to buy into a lifestyle, the American consumer requires more. As he allows them to gratify their need to buy into his personality, he must sometimes ponder whether what is happening is a Calvary or a saintly apotheosis.

PHOTOGRAPHS

MUCH HAVE I TRAVELLED

'She's provincial. People look at her and think, "I'm not sure she's got it right." She's a bit flashy. Quite monumental, though. Her dream is to go to Cairo and stay in the best hotel. Maybe meet King Farouk. Provincial but stylish – village style, North African village style. She had the dressmaker make her a real city outfit and she made the shoes, from the best she could find in the village – leopard, crocodile.... Her dream is to go to all the chic shops and read magazines like *Vogue* and *Glamour*. Her nails are perfect and she's losing a few kilos so that she can marry a rich businessman....'

Manolo Blahnik is doing what he loves to do. He is conjuring the mood of a shoe by creating a story around it. He picks up another, his hand tracing its contours, tilting its heel and running around the straps. 'Now this one', he says, entering a new imaginary world, 'is rather a chic woman. Very influenced by *Marie Claire* and *Elle*. Very French. Very 1968. She's going to Casablanca. In a way, she's quite bourgeois and pretentious. Keeps her house clean. Puts calla lilies on the sideboard. Has friends in Paris. Has a beautiful Maggie Rouff linen suit for the boulevards of Casablanca.'

He stops, attracted by another shoe. '*This* is a shoe for a Mediterranean girl. She could be from Palermo – no, from Naples. Very modern. Very now. She's wearing a little Versace dress in lime. Tits pushed out. The sort of Italian woman who wouldn't even have *existed* two generations, no, even one generation ago....'

Blahnik begins to dart around his office, swooping on the rows of samples and eagerly picking up shoes, talking ever faster all the time: 'This one is called Granada. It's based on a mantilla, or that marvellous ironwork you see in Seville. You know, the grilles on the windows....' Another catches his eye. 'I *love* that one!' he cries, eyes glittering with excitement. 'She's from Jaipur, where she has a marvellous house, all cool colonnades and superbly polished tiles. She's come to Paris and her father has allowed her to bring diamonds from India. A cocotte for our times....'

Sicilian palaces, Balinese temples, South Beach, Isak Dinesen in Africa, Nubian beauties, Somalia, Heidi, Hollywood, Ava Gardner, the Alhambra – 'and this one is very prim and mumsy, very... *Edinburgh*' – the imagination crisscrosses the world and its cultures as Manolo pinpoints influences and moods which have gone into creating his latest collection. As he talks, he turns into a sophisticated Hans Christian Andersen of fashion, spinning witty tales and fairy stories and creating worlds in a few sentences. As he talks, you can see the women and hear the sounds of the streets in Zanzibar, Bombay, Santiago and Rome – 'this is very *dolce vita*, very Anita Ekberg and Anthony Steele fighting the paparazzi in via Veneto'. And, in a simultaneous counter-rhythm, these are the judgements which show that Blahnik knows precisely what he is doing to us and our imaginations when he designs a shoe. For every 'Isn't that divine!' there are other, more interesting, asides: 'Borderline Liz Taylor and Ferragamo on a bad day!' He tosses the sandal aside and picks up another: 'Look at this material. It's tweed! It's bad, but not bad bad.' 'High heels for centurions – I can see a lady from Ankara in these, can't you?'

Another: 'This has sold like…like cookies. Can you imagine!' Always, his great love for what he does shines through. 'Look at this heel', he says, his voice a mixture of pride and tenderness. 'It's like an African spear. It even has a medieval feel.' He runs his finger sensuously up it. 'No, no, really it's totally Africa. This heel is divine. It's great. I love it. Africa! Africa!'

Manolo Blahnik is, like most people who work in fashion, a perennial traveller. It goes with the territory. The fashion business is always in flux. Never static — new talents rise as old ones fade — it is a global concern, ignoring temporal and physical barriers as it moves across the world. It is probably true that, at any moment, at least 5 percent of those who make their living by making fashion will be on an aeroplane or in a meeting that has involved a journey by air. Blahnik probably travels more than most because his business stretches across so many continents. His shoes are all made in Italy. As he creates each last himself and controls every stage in the development and manufacture of a new range, this means many weeks spent in Milan. He normally stays in the same room in the same hotel, living a life of almost monastic monotony, rarely eating anywhere but in the hotel dining room and normally taking only one simple course, such as a risotto or an omelette.

For months of the year, Manolo feels that his life is dominated by timetables, tickets, departure lounges and hire cars. When he goes to America it is to promote the new line, which means he swaps Concorde for flights to Houston, LA, San Francisco and Chicago. In each city he checks into almost identical luxury hotels which are in no sense the way in which he likes to live. Even at holiday times, when he returns to the Canary Islands to see his mother and work on the current collection, he faces yet more departure lounges and boarding gates. He especially hates these flights home because they are full of tourists. Although he recognizes the islands' economic reliance on these visitors, he is horrified at how much they have destroyed of the land and life he knew as a boy. 'It's really time to stop', he claims, 'before everything is destroyed by the developers and everywhere becomes the same, like the coastline of mainland Spain, where nobody who goes there is interested in anything but the beach and the sea.'

Although a reluctant traveller, Blahnik is, perforce, an observant one. No matter how briefly he might be in Madrid or New York, he notices a new mood, a change of attitude, how people are behaving in the streets and what is happening in the restaurants. He instantly clicks into the indigenous life wherever he is because not only does he refuse to think of himself as a tourist — a species he largely abhors — he is rarely treated as one, since his formidable range of languages means he can almost always communicate directly with whomever he meets. He usually has something to communicate because one advantage of being in limbo in an aeroplane for several hours is that Blahnik, a voracious reader, can catch up with newspapers, periodicals and books in English, Italian, French, Spanish and several other European languages. Even when he is not travelling, Blahnik spends hours reading, watching the news on television or rerunning videos of his favourite films.

Far left: An arrangement of objets in a corner of Blahnik's house in Bath, including a drawing by Antonio. Photograph by Michael Roberts.

Left: Cecil Beaton's hat, set off, appropriately enough for the man who changed attitudes to flower arranging, by flowers, with a pair of Manolo zebra-striped slippers to temper the flora with some fauna. Photograph by Michael Roberts.

Right: Classical fragments with feet, human and sculpted. A photograph by Michael Roberts taken in Manolo's house in Bath featuring a photograph by Horst, a gift from Manolo's sister, Evangelina, and her daughter, Kristina.

Like any frequent traveller, Blahnik has favourite places, the cities where he feels most at home. He is always happy in Madrid because he can often squeeze in a trip to the Prado, the museum he most enjoys. He is stimulated in New York and Paris by the exhibitions – 'the best in the world' – finds LA entertaining, but has recently been happiest in the American South. In 1995, as well as visiting the Far East, he took a trip to South Carolina and Georgia, falling in love with Charleston and Savannah. As he told a local newspaper, 'I love the houses, especially in Charleston – very grand, very elegant.' In the same interview he talked about how he attempts to use the gruelling round of travel to bring creative rewards. What he hopes for, and often finds, are 'shocks to the mind, which lead to inspiration for a collection. It can be the edge of a building, the colour of a sky or even just the mood of a city.'

Of all the places in America, it is Texas that feeds his soul, his capacity for wonder and his sense of humour. It is the stop on his promotional tours to which he most looks forward, finding Texan women 'wild and mad – and they don't pretend. They are what they are.' They lionize him, inviting him to grand private dinners in their palatial homes and arranging elegant fork lunches to entertain him. And, of course, he entertains *them*, rising to the sophistication of his audience and throwing off one-liners to everybody's delight. Having been deeply doubtful that America could be a place for him, he has increasingly come to appreciate the unique qualities it possesses. As he explains: 'I love the naivety and freshness of America. It isn't burdened with history as Europe is. I like the Midwest because of the space and the people. And I'm always happy in New York because I'm a medieval person and it is a totally medieval city. People live in towers and they come down to *fight* – for food, for carriages, to sell their wares.'

Manolo Blahnik has always spoken in broad brushstrokes and knows well how to trim an opinion so its slant flatters the listener. He is, after all, the modern equivalent of a sixteenth-century courtier. Much as he extols the joys of America, it is Europe that appeals to such a cultured man, and the Europe of the history books in particular. As he says, 'I'm very Latin. I love the Mediterranean. My favourite countries are Spain and Italy.' It is the latter where he spends most time because that is where the

Page 128: Scrapbook pictures of interests and aspects of Manolo's life, including the books, photographs and personal memorabilia which are such a part of it, photographed in Bath.

Page 129: Photographs of Manolo posing in his Notting Hill flat for Horatio Goni in 1978.

This page: Manolo's mother in front of the house of his grandfather. At one-day old she took Manolo there: their room was on the first floor, to the right of the picture.

factories which make his shoes are located, but it is not the northern cities like Milan that appeal but the decadent ones of the south, in particular Naples and Palermo.

When Manolo Blahnik talks about southern Italian architecture he gets very excited and begins to speak very fast and loud. The effect is as if Sir George Solti were conducting *Taras Bulba* and *Die Meistersinger* simultaneously. Manolo adores the Bourbon kings, because they put such a stamp on southern Italy. As he says, 'Their buildings are majestic and yet monastic. They have a harmony, a wonderful elegance. Caserta is much more powerful than Versailles. It has that southern strength that I find so satisfying. And as for Naples, I get excited every time I go. The buildings are magnificent. I love the people – and the food! It still has an enormous strength as a city. I don't like Capri half as much. Yes, Hadrian's Villa is marvellous and so is Axel Munthe's San Michele, of course. That view across the Bay of Naples to Vesuvius is one of the great vistas of the world. And I love all that decadent Norman Douglas period on Capri but, ultimately, it isn't strong enough for me. Maybe it's because there aren't enough palaces and churches.'

There are plenty of both in Sicily, a place claimed by Manolo to be his spiritual home in Italy. 'Maybe it's because it is an island and I came from an island,' he suggests. 'It is so different from the mainland. I've been there several times and it always grips me. I love the atmosphere. Actually, when I'm in Sicily I want it just to be me and Sicily. I much prefer to travel alone. To me, it is the most beautiful, savage place in the world. Palermo, Agrigento, Catania – these are very special places. I love to stay in the San Domenico Palace in Taormina. It's a very special place for me. They filmed Monica Vitti there for the party scene in *L'Avventura*, with Gabriele Ferzetti. When I first saw the film, I knew I had to find that place. But the whole island is separate and different. The architecture is so sensual.'

Favourites in an island full of favourites are the villas of Bagheria: the Villa Palagonia, with its sculptures of monsters and dwarves, and Villa Valguarnera, with its famous view and garden. They are places to which Manolo would return every year if his schedule allowed – as he would also like to do with Prague, in his opinion the most beautiful and complete city in Europe. 'I regret

Home
May 1987

that I never went to Prague when I was a child', he confesses, 'but the Communist regime made that impossible. But I went with my father in 1980 and he tried to show me what it was like before it became a closed city. It had a powerful effect on me. In a sense it illuminated the missing side of my cultural background.'

Of all the places Manolo has visited, it is England that he has made his home. From the first moment he was bowled over by it and even now can imagine living nowhere else. As he says, 'England is the last refuge for people like me. In England, an eccentric like me feels at ease.' In a sense, the England that first attracted him and still feeds his imagination only really existed – if at all – in the brief, final flowering of the upper classes between the wars. It was the world of the Duke of Windsor, sartorial hero and subconscious mentor in dress for Manolo and, above all, the world of his greatest hero, Cecil Beaton. 'I was possessed by Beaton all through my youth,' he claims. 'I loved his photographs, his drawings and especially his diaries. He was absolutely at the centre of a world which held a huge attraction for me. When I came to London I longed to meet him.'

And the young man did, although by then Beaton had been sadly diminished by a stroke from which he never fully recovered. Blahnik was invited to dinner at the home of a friend. 'I was terrified!' he recalls. 'When I got there I found the other guest was Lady Diana Cooper, another of my great idols. It was extraordinary to be sitting in the same room with the two people who stood for everything I loved about England. Beaton was very chatty, full of sharp questions. He didn't find it too easy to talk. I remember I'd just come back from New York, where I'd seen Angela Lansbury in *Sweeney Todd*. They asked me all about it then Beaton said, "I knew the mother. She was impossible." After dinner, in the drawing room, Lady Diana nodded off. Beaton said, "Poor Diana, she's getting past it." A few minutes later she woke up and the conversation went on. Then Beaton dropped off. Lady Diana turned to us and said, "Poor Cecil, I think he's past it, don't you?"'

Beaton took to Manolo and invited him, along with Barney Wan, art director of British *Vogue*, to his Wiltshire home, Redditch House. It had a great influence on Manolo. He recalls walking through the rooms, each one a perfect example of British

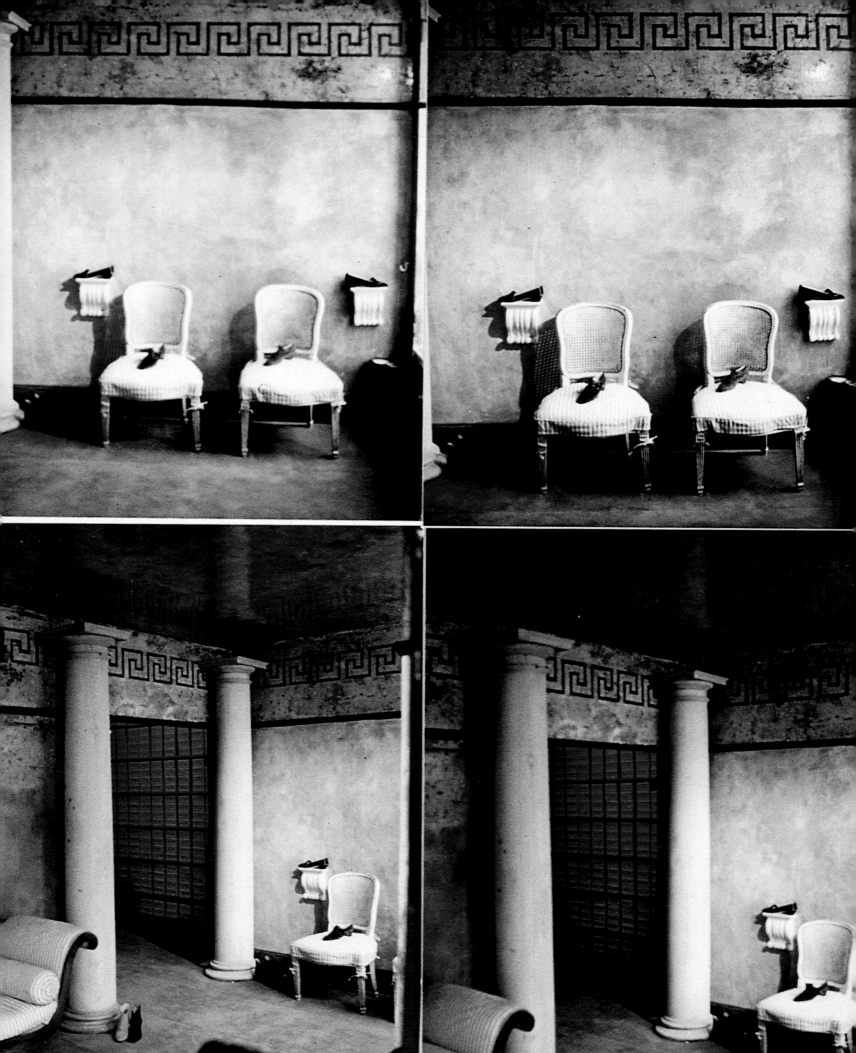

*Manolo looking debonair in the
sort of clothes which have become
his trademark: classic tailoring
frequently enlivened by audacious
deviations from the gentlemanly
sartorial codes, in this case (left) a
waistcoat from Santa Fe.
Photographed in Manolo's Bath
home by Michael Roberts.*

patrician taste, thinking, 'This is exactly how a house should be.' He was thrilled when Beaton agreed to draw some of his shoes for an advertisement. He still has the drawings today and he finds them deeply moving. They were the last things Beaton did before his death. When he received the cheque, he wrote to Manolo saying, 'I'm so glad you like my little commercial'.

As with all travellers, the concept of home is very important to Manolo Blahnik. He has had several in London. One, in Notting Hill, was described by Joan Juliet Buck: 'The apartment of a gentleman, with baronial cupboards full of biographies, paintings of gods and fauns, statues of satyrs, carved beds and chandeliers illuminated with real candles. Here and there he has draped some ticking across a wall because draped curtains, he says, make him happy.' It was a mannered and theatrical setting well suited to Manolo Blahnik in the seventies, although his approach to interior decorating was to deepen and become richer before reaching its apotheosis in his house in Bath – the city Manolo describes as 'an old friend' although he is increasingly appalled by what developers are allowed to do with Britain's last remaining full Georgian town.

Before moving to Bath, Manolo lived in Barnes, but he relocated when he found his perfect townhouse. He discovered it quite by accident in 1982, having gone to Bath because his shoes had been chosen for Bath Costume Museum's 'Dress of the Year' award to complement an outfit by Sheridan Barnett. Strolling around the town which he has subsequently described as the 'last refuge of what England should look like, my childhood idea of England', he fell in love with the Georgian facade the moment he saw it. 'I knew at once I would give anything to have it,' he says.

Remarkably, a little later he saw a picture of the house in an estate agent's window and decided that he *would* have it. He sold the house in Barnes and lost no time in turning his new home into everything he had ever dreamed of: part English country house; part Georgian townhouse; part Visconti set.

Bath and Blahnik were made for each other. 'Bath is heaven for me', he says. 'The stone, the proportions and the feeling of decaying splendour are all perfect for me.' He set about creating a house worthy of Bath at its height, making each room an evocation of the graciousness of upper-class life of the kind Beaton had created in Wiltshire and in his stage and film sets. Eclectic but frankly theatrical, the house was decorated as it was conceived when built in 1786: as a setting for a way of life, a public-private place for display. The fabric of the building was barely touched but Manolo brought in his hundreds of books, casts of Greek and Roman busts, Piranesi prints and photographs and drawings given to him by friends or found in out-of-the-way places, one of his most treasured being a portrait of Serge Lifar which he bought at the Beaton sale in 1980. The furniture included Regency desks and sofas, eighteenth-century Russian chairs, tables designed by Manolo, lamps from Milan, rugs from flea markets – all arranged with setlike perfection to look correct from any angle.

Blahnik had created the perfect setting for a cultured, aesthetic man. Unfortunately, a few years after it was completed the house was subjected to an audacious robbery in which a gang posing as removal men drove up while Manolo was away and removed much that was of value. It was a blow, but it could not destroy the magic of the house. Although many of the things stolen cannot be

Right: Michael Roberts captures the exuberant spirit of Manolo in these 1986 pictures. Could the rhythms have been provided by the Arabian music Manolo has loved since childhood?

Page 143: Manolo photographed in the Beatonesque manner by Michael Roberts in 1992 for Harpers & Queen.

'The apartment of a gentleman, with baronial cupboards full of biographies, paintings of gods and fauns, statues of satyrs, carved beds and chandeliers illuminated with real candles. Here and there he has draped some ticking across a wall because draped curtains, he says, make him happy.'

MANOLO BLAHNIK

replaced, the house still maintains its elegant atmosphere and remains the place where Blahnik feels totally at ease, at one with the city as well as his immediate surroundings. His favourite spot is a chair in front of a window in the first-floor drawing room. When he sits in it he has a view of Bath that is unchanged from the eighteenth century. Nothing of the modern world intrudes.

Blahnik's hand is so sure, his taste so confident, that it is easy to see him as an interior decorator *manqué*. What his homes show clearly is what a fine set designer he would have been had Mrs Vreeland's advice to him been different and he had not become a shoemaker. As it is, he brings the two things together in his shops, which are as exquisite as the shoes sold in them. Old Church Street is tiny and jewel-like, with walls distressed and polished in a re-creation of Pompeii or a Greek villa. Complete with friezes running around the top of the walls, pillars, marble tables and Regency chaise longues, it is, like his homes, a specific evocation of something that never existed outside Manolo's vivid imagination. In that sense, it is more perfect than any possible historic antecedents. Its deliberately contrived sense of temporal decay momentarily halted is far more convincing than the walls of a delapidated English country house or a Sicilian palazzo abandoned to the ravages of time and weather for 200 years.

The shop in Old Church Street has been likened to a boudoir or a dressing room but it is first and foremost a well-orchestrated and efficient selling area that has the elusive ingredient of the very best shops: it is a place of welcome and refuge to which people wish to come and, once there, are reluctant to leave. It perfectly chimes with how Manolo Blahnik is seen in London.

The Blahnik shop in New York is different but, if it is less overtly a display of his creative soul, it represents a clever amalgam conceived to answer the specific needs of the city and its retailing approaches, which are very different from those of Chelsea. A gutted nineteenth-century townhouse on West 54th Street, the store was a reaction as much as a statement. 'I hated our previous New York shop,' Manolo says. 'It was like a horrible Women's Exchange tearoom from the fifties. I wanted this shop to be very different. But New York is not one thing but a fusion of many cultures, styles and moods. I felt we should be more neutral than in London, without slipping into that minimal, undecorated wasteland look of so many shops around the world. It had to be warm and inviting.' It is that simple but inviting quality that he brings to all his shops, including those in the Far East.

Recapturing the spirit of his favourite architecture from Italy, Blahnik opted for the bone colours of the stone of Naples, Venice and Palermo to give a silvery but warm shimmer to the shop. Characteristically, at the last minute he decided something was missing. Hiring a van, he charged around New York buying up African stools to dot around the showroom. It was a masterstroke, creating a space suddenly alive where previously dead, the stools acting as perfect punctuation marks to the story of the overall theme. As he has said, 'Coming to a shop for shoes, the customer should be spoiled, pampered and made to feel as if she's in a temple of pleasure.' It is a measure of the skill of the man that he not only conceives shoes that most women find irresistible, but also places them in a setting so perfect that resistance ceases to be even an academic possibility.

Hiring a van, he charged around New York buying up African stools to dot around the showroom. It was a masterstroke, creating a space suddenly alive where previously dead, the stools acting as perfect punctuation marks to the story of the overall theme. As he has said, 'Coming to a shop for shoes, the customer should be spoiled, pampered and made to feel as if she's in a temple of pleasure.'

PASSION FOR PERFECTION

The man who sometimes seems in interviews to be like a feather blowing in the wind is decisive and clear in the factory, only occasionally expressing doubt in the very early discussions. When he sees a sample he can tell at a glance if something is wrong, whether it is still at last stage or a prototype.

Manolo Blahnik is one of the handful of shoemakers of quality who spanned the twentieth century. He is the last example of that long chain which began before World War I with Yanturni, an academic and intellectual, curator at the Cluny Museum in Paris, who made shoes for a privileged and wealthy clientele, including the great shoe collector, Mrs Rita d'Acosta Lydig. Next in the select line is the Italian, André Perugia, who made shoes for the clients of the legendary couturier Paul Poiret, the man who introduced orientalism to Europe even before Diaghilev and the Ballets Russes caused a sensation in Paris. Perugia indulged in flights of fancy, producing shoes which appealed to the Surrealists and were adored by Elsa Schiaparelli and the clique of eccentrics, including Dali, who clustered around her in Paris. He is Manolo's favourite because of his wit and modernity. 'He was way before his time', he points out.

But there was a commercially better known *bottier* working in Florence before World War II who came into his own as shoemaker to the stars in the fifties. Salvatore Ferragamo, born in poverty in southern Italy, emigrated to America, gravitated to Hollywood and discovered his great skill. His strength lay in his ability to marry the practical with the decorative to make shoes that appealed to all women, from Queen Elizabeth II to Greta Garbo and most women in between. He founded an empire that still flourishes.

Manolo Blahnik's immediate predecessor in this exclusive roll call of shoemaking talent was Roger Vivier, a man of protean inventiveness who worked with Christian Dior in the fifties, producing collections that matched the spirit of Dior's clothes twice a year – and doing it so successfully that his name appeared on the label inside the shoes alongside that of Dior, a unique tribute. In a long working life, Vivier created some of the world's most delicate and decorative shoes, based on his research into the dress of the past.

In a sense, Manolo Blahnik is the son of all these predecessors, taking their skills and achievements to even higher levels in his unique approach to creating shoes. In another sense, he can be seen as the daddy of them all. Unquestionably great though they were, none captured that moment of perfection between practicality and beauty with the aplomb or consistency with which Blahnik has done throughout his career. He continues to do so by setting himself new challenges that give him new opportunities which keep him eternally modern and ahead of his contemporaries. Blahnik has spawned his own school. The world is full of Manolo-wannabes (prophetically taken as the name of a shoe by one of his contemporaries) who make shoes in the Manolo manner as the most natural homage to a master of the craft from those who hope some day to reach his eminence. Flattering as this is for any craftsman, it has its darker side. Blatant copies of Manolo Blahnik's collections are commonplace. They are found in every fashion capital in the world, executed with more or less skill, but always failing to re-create the spirit of the original. How could they do anything other? Does a copy of a Fragonard, no

matter how skilled, convince the expert? Is a Miro pastiche likely to seduce anybody but the artistically gauche?

Flattery is one thing, outright piracy another. As Manolo Blahnik has become a world fashion figure he has become increasingly under siege by people who wish to pillage his ideas and make money from them even before he can. As a creator of the highest artistic integrity, he is distressed by what he regards as blatant theft. 'They try to steal the ideas even when they are still at the earliest stage of manufacture, when we are finalizing the last. People phone the factory, asking for details, claiming to work for me. There are men who even obtain jobs by saying they worked for me as assistant designers.'

To anyone who knows anything of the Blahnik organization, the claim is absurd. Manolo Blahnik is a one-man band as a designer. He alone creates a collection. His sister Evangelina, who is in charge of the European aspects of the business, and his American business partner, George Malkemus, join him in Italy, where all his shoes are made, in order to choose with him the colours and fabrics appropriate for their specific markets. There are no design assistants, colour coordinators or stylists in the Manolo Blahnik organization, as there have never been, even at the very beginning. All creative decisions are Blahnik's alone.

That being so, some doors can always be opened by a telling chink if the money is right. It doesn't take long for a pirate with a camera or a good visual memory to take advantage of a fleeting moment in order to discover how the designer's mind is working at a particular time. We are not talking here of the copyists who take pictures of the shoes in shop windows. That is a form of flattery which is relatively harmless, as the collection is finished and in the clear commercial light of day. The covert photograph is the one that endangers Blahnik's company. As he says, if the copyist gets his version of a new season's look in the shops before Blahnik does, or even simultaneously, this is potentially deeply damaging. Pirated versions of shoes can always be knocked up more quickly than the real thing because a genuine Manolo Blahnik is handmade at all points, inevitably a slower process than the machine-making of the copy.

For those with sophisticated eyes, the difference is palpable. I have seen many 'knock-offs' of Manolo Blahnik's shoes in the course of researching this book and, even to an eye which is not expert in female footwear, the copies are invariably and obviously inferior. Some copies are so crude that it is impossible even to

imagine whom they might convince: certainly, nobody who has ever held a Blahnik original, balanced in the palm of a hand nor, I am assured by the women who wear the real thing, anybody who has ever walked more than a couple of paces in a pair. But there are many clever craftsmen in the world and it is possible, if time and money are expended, to make 'rip-off' Blahniks which are neither crude nor crass but are able to capture some of the essence of the original.

No forger could capture more than a fraction of the spirit and genius that inform the genuine product, something totally unreproducible by any copyist. The quality of a Blahnik shoe is built into the creative process and cannot be separated from the man, as becomes apparent to any observer who visits the factories in Italy where all the production is done. It is only when you've watched the women stitching straps by hand and men carefully gluing soles together under the watchful, even paternalistic, Blahnik eye, that you begin to realize why Blahnik's shoes can never be cheap if they are to retain their unique quality, just as a Lamborghini or a *premiere cru* can never be cheap and still retain the qualities for which they are famed. Blahnik is tired of explaining this. As he says: 'When you realize the kind of work that goes into my shoes and then see what you are expected to pay for all these referential versions' – his kind expression for what those of cruder minds would call rip-offs – 'then they are actually cheap, rather than too expensive.'

There is a considerable degree of logic in this contention. A good Blahnik pastiche will sell for over £200, while the original is not necessarily very much more expensive. But, as Blahnik points out, 'Most of these copies are rubbish shoes, made of cardboard. They always cut corners to make a quick profit!' His voice rises in incredulity and disbelief. He can genuinely see no point in such a course of action. 'It's all so derivative. And they even go back to the past to steal my old ideas from magazines. It's grotesque! It's fashion necrophilia.' As Woody Hochswender pointed out in *Harper's Bazaar* of August 1995, it is all part of the 'frenzy for great shoes…which is why a minor industry of Blahnik copycats has been thriving. Relatively speaking, it's comparatively easy to copy a shoe…from a photo scanned into a computer.' What comes out the other end is in no sense a Blahnik shoe. Made of cheap plastic and inferior leather, it fools no woman of taste – but that does not mean that a comparatively raw approximation of the original cannot damage the probity of the real thing.

The quality of a Blahnik shoe is built into the creative process and cannot be separated from the man, as becomes apparent to any observer who visits the factories in Italy where all the production is done.

When you realize the kind of work that goes into my shoes and then see what you are expected to pay for all these referential versions' – his kind expression for what those of cruder minds would call rip-offs – 'then they are actually cheap, rather than too expensive.'

To find out what makes Manolo Blahnik, in the words of US *Vogue* in October 1977, 'far and away the most inventive, witty and iconoclastic *bottier* working today', it is necessary to watch him at work. The processes of conceiving, creating and selling a Manolo Blahnik collection has the man himself at the centre of each one to a surprising degree. Blahnik delegates nothing to do with the creative process, not even bringing the message to the customer.

The process starts with the drawings. Feathery, soufflé-light concoctions, they look as if they have flown through an open window and alighted on the page, so full are they of movement and deft delineation. Watching Blahnik work, one is overcome by the unfairness of life. It really should not be this easy. He dashes the drawings off with spirit and skill, barely having to pause for thought. One after another, they pour out of his fertile brain. 'I'm not from that design school of opening magazines to get ideas. Ideas come to me constantly. I have to edit them down all the time. It's as much a torment as it is a gift,' he points out. He talks as he draws, explaining what is in his mind. You suspect that he probably also talks when he's alone drawing, the creative process so completely takes control of him. As he slides a drawing to one side, ready to start immediately on the next, it becomes clear that this is a continuous process, where one idea gives rise to at least six more. It is as near to seamless as it could be.

In all the speed and amazing manual dexterity – firm, assured, expansive hand movements, followed by precise, sharp little jabs as the details are fitted in – what impresses the onlooker is how complete this two- or three-minute process is. As Blahnik hands over a drawing with a deprecating laugh you realize that you have a complete shoe before you in a drawing not merely conveying the spirit, as fashion sketches traditionally do, but also delineating the detail. It is a mood drawing and a practical, almost technical drawing at the same time, from which it is perfectly possible to visualize and even make the actual shoe.

Blahnik needs no studio or special desk. He draws in his office in London, at his home in Bath and at his factories in Italy. All he requires to initiate the creative process is a sketchbook, his Tombo Japanese brush pens, a flat surface – and a degree of peace. A natural draughtsman, he makes the act of drawing, and the job of creating, seem simple. But it is when the process moves to the next stage, with the preparation of the lasts, that the most surprising side of Blahnik is revealed. Beneath the elegant exterior of the international *boulevardier* is a craftsman, at his happiest when in his factories working alongside his bands of skilled artisans.

All Blahnik's shoes are made in Italy, in factories in the north of the country where he finds the standards of artisanal workmanship of the highest. There are two factories in the Vigevano district, about one and a half hour's drive from Milan, and two in Parabiago, which is slightly nearer to the centre. It is in these *ambiente* that the true Manolo Blahnik comes alive. 'I love working in the factories', he claims, and it is perfectly clear that he does, merely from the way in which he bends down to talk, in fluently idiomatic Italian, to a worker; or from the excitement with which he picks up the latest sample, minutely examining it for design faults or imperfections in execution. Above all, it is apparent in the quiet pride that takes hold of him at the end of a day as he watches a batch of shoes being packed ready for shipment.

Blahnik spends several weeks at the factories twice a year, creating, making and supervising his collections. For a man who constantly travels, whose permanent cry is 'I never have time!', they are a biannual watershed where he is able to stop rushing from one place to another, finally able to concentrate on one thing at a time. Or rather, on many things, but all with one focus: the collection.

I observed Manolo at one of the factories in Parabiago, a typically Italian scene. Behind the high metal gates, automatically operated from inside, the factory is a sterile grey block of the sort found in thousands on the outskirts of Italian cities, surrounded by post-fifties villas which still keep some links to the country culture they have dispersed. From Manolo's office can be seen chickens roaming at random below washing lines. Inside, the factory is strictly utilitarian, with concrete floors which in the winter defy all attempts to warm the place. This is where Manolo Blahnik works for seven days a week – and he never begrudges the time.

Blahnik's is a close-knit family firm in the traditional Italian manner, with the owner and his brother in charge of the shopfloor and his married daughter acting as Manolo's right hand and general factotum. The two have a rapport which makes for a very close working relationship as he explains what is required and she ensures that it is done. The man who sometimes seems in

interviews to be like a feather blowing in the wind is decisive and clear in the factory, only occasionally expressing doubt in the very early discussions. When he sees a sample he can tell at a glance if something is wrong, whether it is still at last stage or a prototype. 'I need this enlarged…higher here', he says, pointing. His colleagues understand immediately. 'Si, troppo pesante (too heavy)', they nod. Their admiration for Blahnik is evident. As one says to me, when he has been called downstairs to look at a sample, 'He's not just a stylist. He's also a technician and that's why he is such a success.'

Explain to me how you spend your days, I ask him. 'Days!' Blahnik flashes back. 'Are you kidding? I don't have days. I have minutes. Everything is rush.' Then he laughs. 'This is my spiritual home. I've been coming for twenty-five years. I always feel good here. They do everything I ask.' The process has begun in Bath long before Manolo arrives in Italy. His drawings and proposals for the lasts are sent ahead of him, so that as soon as he arrives at the factory he can get down to work immediately. 'My tools are age-old,' he points out. 'Files, sandpaper, knives, scissors, hammers and pins. I'm not a computer man. I must touch and know. The people downstairs treat the machines as if they were gold. They love them. Not me.'

Blahnik can spend a whole day carving a single last, normally out of beech, and for him the body of the shoe is as subtle and aerodynamic as the hull of a yacht or the prow of an airliner. Infinite care is taken to ensure that it is perfect before it goes to production stage. At this point Blahnik is thinking on two levels: on one he is a sculptor, on the other an engineer. It is a question of aesthetics and aerodynamics as he carves, cuts and sands until the shape is precisely what he requires. But it is the heel above all that shows the unique Blahnik skills. If any part of a shoe can be said to be more important than the others, it is the heel: not only because it is the first and most obvious marketing device but also because on it will depend the whole balance and ultimate comfort of the shoe.

The heel is also the shoe's most vulnerable feature because, although the hardest part to create, demanding a mind that works to the millimetre, it is also the easiest to rip off – and the most important, as it says more clearly than anything else, 'this season's Manolo'. Shoes are erotically charged objects and in a Blahnik shoe the charge is found in sexy little strips, delicious bows, marcasite clasps but, above all, in the rhythm of the heel as it swoops down to the floor, following the parabola the designer has perfected to a degree of subtlety that his competitors, working to a price as they always do, would find incomprehensible.

This is what makes Manolo Blahnik such a privileged exception. He owns the firm and therefore controls his own name. He can spend as much time as he requires to produce something of which he is proud, something over which he can exclaim, 'I get excited by my shoes'. And that is what is important, not the costs of production or the prices charged in the shop. Every shoe must please Blahnik's exacting eye. It is an eye that he has honed over the years to give perfect focus. 'I have the advantage of study,' he points out. 'I've been studying the art of the shoe – I'm sorry, I know that sounds pretentious, but I can't put it any other way – studying for over twenty years. I know every process. I know how to cut and cut away here,' he caresses the side of the shoe he is holding, 'and still make it so that it stays on the foot.' He points to the toes, 'And the secret of toe-cleavage – a very important part of the sexuality of the shoe. You must only show the first two cracks. And the heel. Even if it's twelve centimetres high it still has to feel secure – and that's a question of balance. That's why I carve each heel personally myself – on the machine and then by hand with a chisel and file, until it is exactly right.'

It is then that the lasers are brought in to make any minute corrections that might be required. When the last is perfect an aluminium mould is made of it, which is then used to make the plastic lasts on which the shoes will actually be made. It is when you see and feel these plastic shapes that you understand Blahnik's contention that he is an architect manqué. As he says, 'I can conceive space, volume and form. And that's the reason I can dream things that actually work. I am essentially a practical man.' Many would consider such a comment too modest, preferring to call Blahnik a practical poet.

Blahnik can spend a whole day carving a single last, normally from beech, and for him the body of the shoe is as subtle and aerodynamic as the hull of a yacht. Infinite care is taken to ensure that it is perfect before it goes to production. At this point Blahnik is thinking on two levels, as a sculptor and as an engineer. It is a question of aesthetics and aerodynamics as he carves, cuts and sands until the shape is precisely what he requires. But it is the heel that shows the unique Blahnik skills.

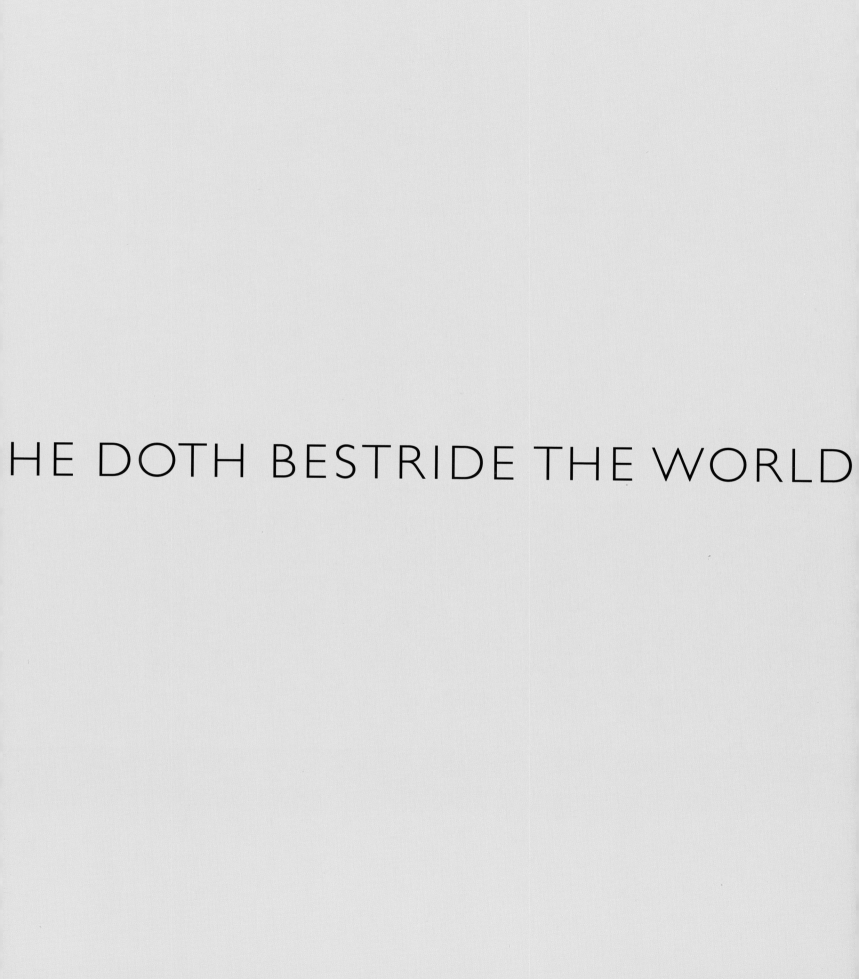

HE DOTH BESTRIDE THE WORLD

A month before *Footwear News* featured a Manolo Blahnik shoe as 'the most talked-about shoe in London' in 1973, the shoemaker was interviewed by his friend Michael Roberts for a magazine feature called 'The Groom at the Top Men'. Photographed by another friend, Eric Boman, Manolo looks matinée-idol *soigné*, as if he were acting in a film by his favourite director Luchino Visconti. But what gives the page its retrospective interest is that, above the details of Blahnik's grooming regime, the text identifies him as 'Writer and Photographer Manolo Blahnik, aged 29: Ultra-chic, Lives in London.'

Was this a little game by two men whose sense of humour still perfectly chimes and who can giggle like mischievous schoolboys over wordplay worthy of the lower school or was Manolo still in two minds as to his real career? Did he even then consider shoe design merely one of the areas in which he might work? Thanks to Roberts and *The Sunday Times*' fashion director, Molly Parkin, who adored Blahnik's exuberant, tangential approach, Manolo's photographs had certainly appeared in the newspaper, featuring the sort of newsworthy names papers always chase and people like

Manolo always make sure they know. In his case he had a three-card flush: Paloma Picasso, Bianca Jagger and Tina Chow. The photographs are stylish and dramatic. Clearly, he had learned much from his friend Eric Boman, who was already making a name for himself as a photographer whose work appeared often in the pages of *Vogue*.

Manolo is vague about this period, although he recalls writing fashion and social stories predominantly for Italian *Vogue*, due again to a social contact, his friend Anna Piaggi. What is not in doubt is the fact that those early years in the seventies were not only the period when Manolo was learning the craft of shoe-making, they were the time when he was forging the fashion personality that was to give him a world profile in years to come. If proof were needed of his growing gilt-edged insider status, it is found on the cover of British *Vogue* for January 1974: a picture of Manolo and Angelica Huston, taken by David Bailey as part of a seventeen-page fashion and holiday piece photographed in the south of France and Corsica and including a shot of the models with Helmut Newton. Blahnik appears on every page.

Later that year, in an interview with his friend Peter Lester, Manolo talked of this modelling role and many other things in a way that was at once endearingly arrogant, engagingly confrontational and, above all, ironic. This is Manolo Blahnik at his most lively, cocky and assured, able to send himself up and laugh at the very things which were making him a talked-about figure in the world of fashionable London. Ironic and provocative, he plunges straight in at the deep end, joking 'I suppose you are going to call me a shoe designer…I am not. I'm the best, the best, the best shoe designer in the world, but a shoe designer I am not.' When Lester asks him about being on the cover of *Vogue*, Blahnik flashes back: 'Not only on the cover. In the whole issue, darling…. I was a VIP model…they were going to use my name, which is good publicity for my shoes.'

Talking of his own photographs, Manolo says he has only been taking them for a year but that they have already been published by French and Italian *Vogue*. He then goes on to talk of his working life: 'I have to be working all the time. I can't stop. I work twenty-four hours a day.' He admits, however, that he takes time

out for some fun. 'I enjoy parties', he says. 'When I go to a party I really give myself a good time. If others enjoy it too, good.' Twenty-five years later the reaction to this curriculum vitae for a life to come can only be *plus ça change*…. Manolo Blahnik is still a workaholic and still enjoys a good time, when he can make space for it in a tightly structured schedule.

The seventies were the formative years for Blahnik, a time in which he laid the foundations for the successes to come. As early as February 1972, *Vogue* was featuring his shoes, sometimes only under the name of Zapata but with increasing frequency as 'Manolo Blahnik for Zapata' or 'Zapata's suede boots by Manolo Blahnik'. The small shop in Chelsea was becoming the place for fashion journalists such as *Vogue*'s Young Ideas editor, Marit Allen, to watch. It was a shop that not only attracted fashion editors like Grace Coddington and Mandy Claperton at *Vogue* but also high-profile women of style, such as Jane Birkin, Charlotte Rampling and Marisa Berenson as its customers. The shoes were already becoming cult objects, attracting visitors passing through London so that a morning at Zapata was built in to the itineraries of the

likes of Lauren Bacall, who at that time bought many clothes from Jean Muir and was frequently in London, and wealthy fashionables from LA to Jakarta.

Manolo Blahnik and his wares were increasingly in demand. After the *succes de scandale* of the runway shoes for Ossie Clark it might have been expected that designers would steer clear of the young shoemaker, but the undeniable originality and wit of his approach were far more attractive than the technical problems were off-putting. In fact, Blahnik – always a fast learner and much more commercially minded than he felt was good for his public image – had soon taken steps to ensure that his shoes would never again be found technically lacking. He was in business, in every sense.

With a loan of £2,000, Blahnik bought out the owner of Zapata so that he could have complete control of all aspects of the firm. His success was so instant that he paid the money off in less than three years and was able to maintain in an interview with *Tatler and Bystander*: 'This is my business. No one has backed me ever, ever, ever.' Although the years of making big money were

far ahead, he was financially secure and supremely confident in his position in the market. 'This shop makes a statement,' he went on. 'I'm not interested in opening a hundred branches or allying myself to bigger businesses – they adulterate your product....You have to produce junk in order to make money. The shop is the only way I can express myself and it changes every month, so it's not very profitable but I don't want to be much bigger than I am now.' The only other outlet he permitted was Browns in South Molton Street, newly opened by his ex-employer, Mrs Burstein, a woman whose taste he admired and whose business skills he hoped to emulate.

Blahnik was able to maintain this stance of exclusivity until the early eighties as far as his own shop was concerned. Meanwhile, undeterred by what Blahnik described in 1988 as the most memorable items from his Ossie Clark collection – 'orange stack heels, rubber heels and fruit ankle-straps: they were disgusting!' – designers began to court him to design and make shoes to complement their collections. A distinct pattern emerged early and has hardly changed.

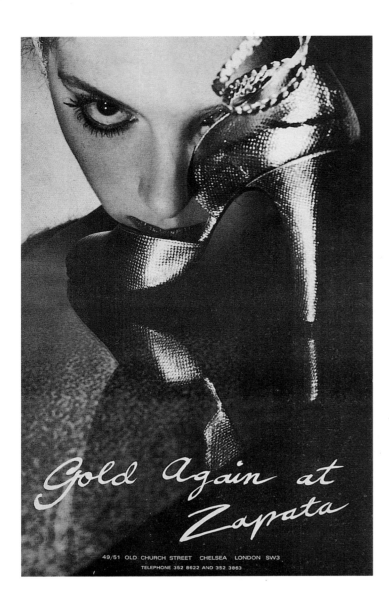

Gold Again at
Zapata

49/51 OLD CHURCH STREET CHELSEA LONDON SW3
TELEPHONE 352 8622 AND 352 3863

There are three ways in which Manolo Blahnik provides shoes for dress designers and couturiers. They may choose shoes from his current range and simply use them on their runways. They may commission him to create designs for their runways that they will sell with the Blahnik label. Or they may commission shoes for the show that go into production and will effectively be sold as their own shoe range, bearing their label rather than Blahnik's. Manolo has no difficulty in working to all three briefs and he has done so highly successfully at every level, something his friend André Leon Talley puts down to his essential pragmatism: 'Manolo has a gothic mind', he says, 'but he lives in today's world. When women wear his shoes, their feet can be both in the clouds and on concrete.' It was this practicality that turned the shop in Old Church Street into a cult temple where, tiny as it was, women flocked to worship in a quasi-religious devotion that would eventually become a global obsession.

In a sense, Blahnik was lucky in that what could conceivably have remained a cottage industry blossomed remarkably quickly into a full-blown commercial concern as he was asked to design shoes for mass-manufacturers and more exclusive designers alike. While continuing to produce shoes for Ossie Clark's shows and the Zapata range, he added to his list of clients Jean Muir but, most importantly, also began to work for the mass-market, youth-oriented fashion firm Fiorucci, the perfect outlet for his exuberant, colourful flights of fancy. It was a mutually productive partnership. Fiorucci customers loved the high-style fashion input he gave the shoes and Manolo loved the financial security that came from working with one of the most commercially successful labels of the seventies. Even more, he loved – and took full advantage of – the opportunity to learn the practicalities and sub-tleties of his trade from the visits he made to the manufacturer's factories in Italy. This was the hands-on experience he required. The more he learned, the stronger and more individual his design signature became.

Manolo Blahnik was a rarity in British fashion in the seventies. Eager to take on the world and learn from it, he was not as insular as most London designers at the time. Further, he was already beginning to make the first moves toward a fashion revo-

lution which, although minor, was important in what it would say about *fin de siècle* fashion developments and of which he was the sole author. In the last two decades of the twentieth century, there have been several significant shifts in the axes of fashion but none more so than the repositioning of accessories in the fashion hierarchy. In the past, shoes were an important element in the appearance of a woman of fashion but their place was tightly proscribed. Unlike millinery, footwear rarely made any statement other than one subservient to the overall concept of a look. In this, they were on the level of handbags, scarves or even gloves. Manolo Blahnik's fashion achievement is to have made the accessory a powerful element in fashion and shoes the most important of all accessories.

His achievement goes further. For most of the twentieth century, shoes have followed the fashion trend set by couturiers. It was Manolo Blahnik who gave them their independence. The man who has always maintained that what he does is outside fashion, and even beyond it, has been proved right. In the nineties, the merchandising equation of decades was finally overturned.

Women no longer bought shoes after they had purchased the other elements of their wardrobe, motivated mainly by the importance of choosing footwear of a style and colour that would 'go' with the rest. Instead, they bought their Manolo Blahniks first and then bought the dress that would fit in with the shoes. Footwear had become the supreme statement in fashionable appearance, saying more about the wearer than all but the most extreme fashion designer's creations. As Manolo has said, 'Women need whimsical accessories to help their boring little black dress to stand out.'

Blahnik's achievement – and it must be considered as an achievement – has to be assessed in the context of what happened in fashion in general during the nineties, because the new approach did not come about in a vacuum. As designers became more extravagant in their creations, so the women who wore them became more practical. But, even as the flights of fancy from London and Paris became increasingly less wearable, the women for whom they went too far were stimulated to want to achieve some controlled madness in their appearance without

STEPS!

FRESH!

FRESH!

JUST LAID!

looking bizarre or laughable or both. It was shoes, and especially the shoes of Manolo Blahnik, that answered the need and rapidly became cult objects. A San Francisco socialite spoke for many Blahnik customers when, in an interview in the nineties, she explained, 'I never throw away any of his shoes. The shoes I have on are over six years old and they still feel fabulous. More important, they make me feel sexy.'

As far back as 1980, the designer had explained the dual approach that would lead to his shoes becoming world leaders, bought compulsively by fashionable women and copied by shoe designers everywhere: 'I have always tried to create in two ways. Throughout the year I produce occasional avant-garde looks for the affluent few…and, twice yearly, winter and summer, I do several designs that are good solid looks that will wear forever. My "commercial" shoes are not really fashion in the sense of wearing a look one season and throwing it away the next. Good basic design just keeps going. My Sabrina slipper, for example, is still one of my all-time bestsellers. The customers like the classics. That's why they remain in production. My crazy and creative designs will not matter to most of my customers but I don't want it thought

that I'd prefer to create for the few rather than the many. I want to see every woman in my shoes….'

Blahnik had begun to lay the groundwork for such an empire when he started to work with Fiorucci, an experience he recalls as 'sandals in Jello colours and high heels in fake leopard – an extremely liberating experience for my imagination'. There were other formative moments, not least the opportunity to see his shoes walking down the runway of Yves Saint Laurent, the couturier whom Blahnik most reveres, even putting him ahead of his beloved Balenciaga and Chanel as far as elegance and sophistication are concerned.

The shoes made by the Italian firm Rossetti were not put into production, being considered too extravagant to make in any number, but that didn't concern Blahnik. Many designers in the late seventies and eighties used his shoes to add style to their runways, including Bill Blass, Caroline Herrera and Geoffrey Beene. This trick of winning approval from designers able to create their own shoes or take examples from the ranges of shoemakers anywhere in the world was as important for raising Blahnik's profile within the fashion industry as the endorsement of

head-to-toe flattery...
brilliant

frills...

pale lit up make-up,
crimson lips and nails...
scent at your ankles,
bracelets,
glamour sandals

Gold hairs-breadth chain
interlocked with diamond hearts,
ankle bracelet; £540, at Cartier.
White and scarlet sandals,
Manolo Blahnik, £25, at Zapata.
Shops, sizes, colours,
see Stockists

Cutex tender loving care
for toenails—Cuticle Cream,
Cuticle Remover
and new Hollyhock Creme Polish.
Tend them as you would
your fingernails
for pretty summer feet,
and pumice away dead skin
on soles and ankles.

Scent all-over—at the back
of knees, ringed round ankles.
Try Prince Matchabelli's
summery Cachet, cool at first,
warming to rich flower scents

women such as Madonna, Diana Ross and Gwyneth Paltrow was for the public at large.

Not that high-profile celebrities ever actually sang 'Manolo' from the rooftops. They didn't need to. Blahnik had reached such a world-class level that it could be taken as read that the women boarding Concorde, walking the red carpet at a gala or being presented with an award would almost certainly be wearing 'Manolos' – a term that has become generic for sexy, diaphanous, high-heeled shoes. The customer with the highest profile of all was, of course, Diana, Princess of Wales, who bought shoes regularly, but not exclusively, from Blahnik, visiting the shop in Old Church Street usually without warning and always without ceremony. Like most of her young contemporaries, the Princess of Wales had become a Blahnik customer when she was still a single girl about town, Lady Diana Spencer, buying at the sale like her girlfriends. When she became a member of the royal family, she continued to buy from Manolo, usually choosing styles from the current range but sometimes asking if she could have a special colour to go with the clothes she would be wearing for future occasions, informal as well as official. She is remembered fondly in

the shop for her informality and sense of humour, her total modesty and lack of grandeur.

The same enthusiasm shown by Manolo's young customers on both sides of the Atlantic was reflected in a more formal way in the citation in the programme for the Committee of the Fashion Designers of America Awards for 1997, when Manolo Blahnik was honoured for the third time, having received a CFDA Special Award in 1987 and the award for Outstanding Excellence in Accessory Design in 1990. The 1997 citation read, in part: 'Blahnik has done for footwear what Worth did for the couture, making slippers into objects of desire, collectibles for women for whom Barbies are too girlish and Ferraris not girlish enough…an incredible piston in the engine of fashion, there is almost no designer he has not collaborated with, no designer who has not turned to him to transform a collection into a concert.'

Blahnik has been performing this runway *legerdemain* for a long time. He worked with Perry Ellis in the early eighties, producing shoes for the fashion shows of the man who many would claim as one of the most original and gifted designers in America and who exerted an influence on fashion across the world. Manolo

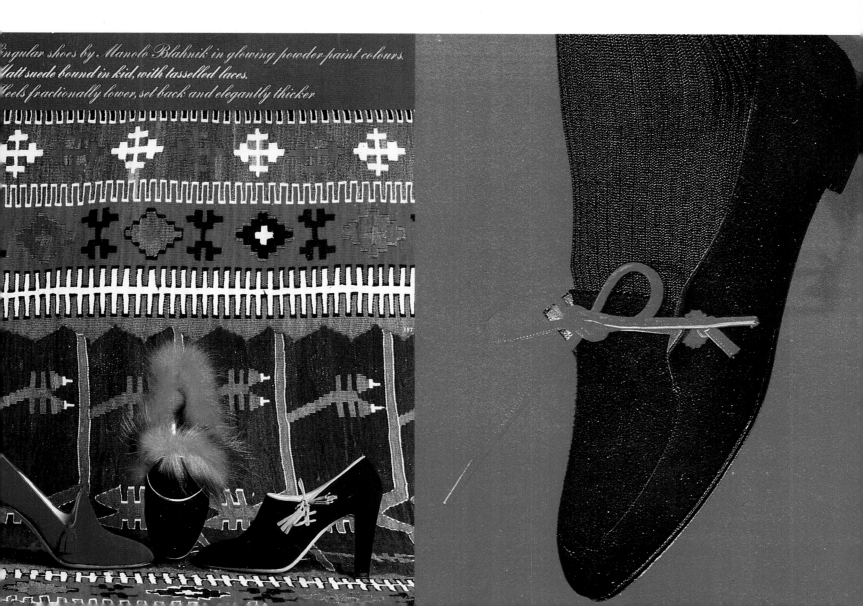

Angular shoes by Manolo Blahnik in glowing powder-paint colours. Matt suede bound in kid, with tasselled laces. Heels fractionally lower, set back and elegantly thicker

*t*here's something brilliant afoot at Manolo Blahnik, who designed this re-think of the classic desert boot for Isaac Mizrahi's New York Collection. It's proved an instant best-seller. Mr Blahnik says, ''It's the youngest shoe I've done in years. It's one of those things that's been there for ages, but which nobody thought of doing in colour, as fashion, before. It's very modern and everybody loves it.'' Fuchsia suede lace-up boot, £180, at Manolo Blahnik, 49-51 Old Church St, SW3. Socks, from a selection, at branches of Sock Shop. Red suede trousers, £745, at Polo Ralph Lauren, 143 New Bond St, W1. Shocking pink suede gloves, £105, at Saint Laurent Rive Gauche, 113 New Bond St, W1. Sizes, colours, see Fashion Information >460

EAMONN J. McCABE

458

Beach-brilliant colors, THIS PAGE: The season's sexy stiletto heels shine brightly on an array of patent leather mules. Manolo Blahnik shoes, about $415 each. Bergdorf Goodman; Manolo Blahnik, NYC. OPPOSITE PAGE: Even beach towels get in the swim, with fish prints in pumped-up pastel tones. Hermès towels, about $180 each. Hermès stores. Details, see In This Issue.

Pages 166–169: One of the reasons why Manolo's Church Street shop has for so long been a site of pilgrimage for sophisticated women is that it is so unlike most shops. Manolo's relaxed 'drawing room' approach to retailing in the eighties was trailblazing and has been followed at all levels. 'Shoes in a setting' was a simple and highly effective idea and the windows pulled customers in as much as the merchandise did. Droll and self-deprecating, they were just witty enough to avoid seeming camp or arch, as these scrapbook pictures show (along with personal ones of Evangelina, Manolo's mother and his niece).

Pages 170–171: Photographers find Manolo Blahnik's shoes stimulating and challenging: are they to be treated as a form of sculpture, fine art or totally utilitarian objects? The solutions here to the conundrum are, from left to right, by David Bailey, Lothar Schmid, Michael Williams and Terence Donovan.

Pages 172–173: As others see him: Four interpretations of Manolo shoes by some of the master photographers of the last twenty years: far left: Eamon J. McCabe for British Vogue, 1988; left: Oberto Gili for US Vogue, 1994; bottom left: Steven Meisel for Italian Vogue, 1995; below: Nick Knight for French Vogue, 1995.

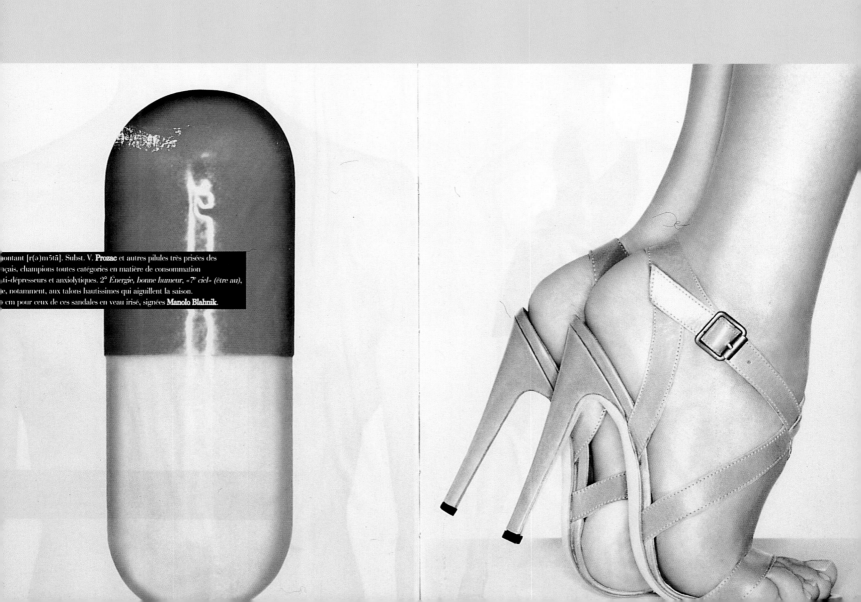

ontant [r(ə)m5tã]. Subst. V. **Prozac** et autres pilules très prisées des
çais, champions toutes catégories en matière de consommation
ti-dépresseurs et anxiolytiques. 2° Énergie, bonne humeur, «7° ciel» (être au),
e, notamment, aux talons hautissimes qui aiguillent la saison.
cm pour ceux de ces sandales en veau irisé, signées **Manolo Blahnik**.

ES
magazine

20 OCTOBER 1995

FASHION ISSUE
LONDON

THE SUNDAY REVIEW

LONDON
FASHION WEEK

How to spot the
Next Big Thing
before it happens

Pearce Fionda
in your wardrobe for
the cost of a stamp

**Who are all
these people?**
Your guide to the
newcomers of the
British fashion scene

**The London
Lowdown**
Deep dish from
behind the catwalk

UNLEASHED

FASHION GOES BANANAS
FIRST OF THE SUMMER FRUIT

GENETICS: BIOLOGY'S BRAVE NEW WORLD

ZOË HELLER MEETS CHARLES MOORE

PLUS THE REHABILITATION OF JAMES STIRLING, GERMANY'S
ONLY POP STAR AND WILLIAM LEITH ON MODERN ART

Left and right: 'Manolos' win readers. Editors have discovered time and again that a Blahnik creation provides a striking cover image. Shoes sell magazines and periodicals because their message is frequently an overtly sexy one, as the pictures here make clear. Homer and Marge Simpson are testimony to the other great quality of Manolo's shoes – their capacity for humour.

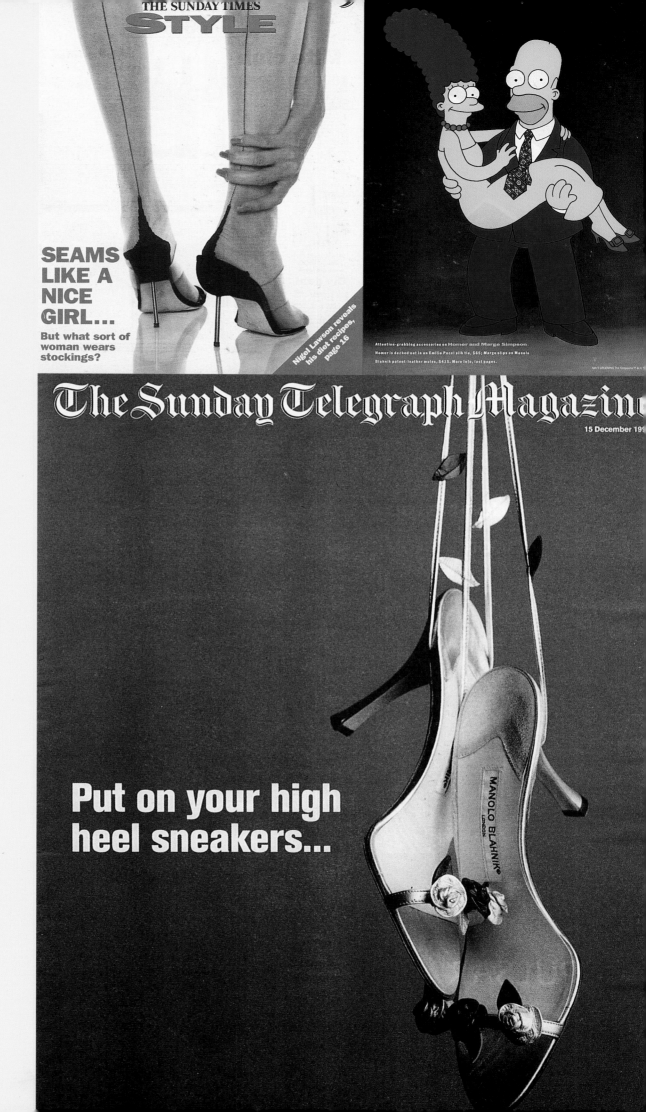

THE SUNDAY TIMES
STYLE

SEAMS LIKE A NICE GIRL...

But what sort of woman wears stockings?

Nigel Lawson reveals his diet recipes, page 16

Attention-grabbing accessories on Homer and Marge Simpson: Homer is decked out in an Emilio Pucci silk tie, $65; Marge slips on Manolo Blahnik patent-leather mules, $415. More info, last pages.

The Sunday Telegraph Magazine

15 December 199

Put on your high heel sneakers...

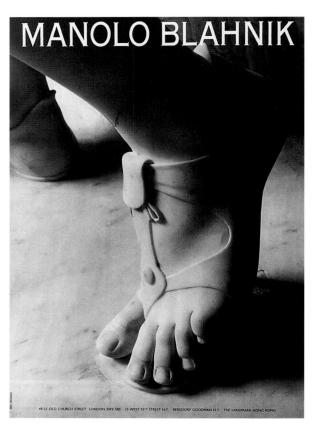

Far left: Bruce Weber, a friend whose photographic work Blahnik much admires, created this picture especially for the bottier – with a little cooperation from his young nephew, who posed for it especially.

Left: An Eric Boman photograph of a classical sculpture of a sandalled foot, used in Blahnik publicity in the nineties.

Right: What it's all about: the bare bones and essence of a Blahnik boot revealed in 1994 in a striking Nick Knight photograph.

remembers the cooperation with fondness. He and Ellis came from the same creative soil and understood each other's approach so perfectly that he considers this one of his most fruitful collaborations. Blahnik considers that its great value after the experience of working with an Italian manufacturer was to open up the American attitude to him, as well as teaching him the differences in approach between the two on the practical level of the factory, a study in different technical cultures which has always fascinated him.

The experience also went some way to breaking down Manolo's reluctance to get more involved with the American market. As he confessed in an interview in 1984, 'I was afraid I might lose my identity in such a vast place.' By then, however, Manolo had begun working with Calvin Klein, an influential experience that began with making shoes for the designer's runway shows but developed into a mutually beneficial business arrangement whereby Manolo's designs were put into production and sold as part of an overall Klein look. It was the first time since Fiorucci that Blahnik had dipped his toe into the pond of mass-marketing. Not only did he survive the shock, he also learned a great deal about production. The shoes themselves were made in southern Italy and, as is his custom, Manolo spent time in the country making each first sample by hand. In addition, he was required to make frequent trips to New York to discuss colours,

shapes and moods with Klein and his design teams, often, as Manolo now recalls, taking a trip on Concorde merely to finalize 'a particular shade of beige'. It was demanding work but, as he had with other designers and manufacturers with whom he worked, Manolo was continually adding to his technical knowledge by studying the lasts, becoming aware of the tensions in different qualities of leather and noticing how seams ran in order to be easily produced on conveyor belts churning out shoes by the thousand weekly.

As a multifaceted designer capable of working to the highest standards at various levels, Manolo Blahnik was increasingly in demand as the eighties folded into the nineties. Always attracted to the vitality and energy of young talent, he was happy to work with emerging talents – often for no financial reward – provided he was convinced that they had the 'spark'. Wherever he found this elusive quality, he was more than ready to help young designers not only by lending shoes or even designing specially for them but also by supporting them by his presence at the show. This endorsement carries great kudos as Blahnik picks with great care the shows to attend, knowing that by sitting in the front row he confers a subtle seal of approval. His choice of words to describe young designers with whom he works is significant of the slightly avuncular approach he habitually takes to them; they are 'the children' or 'the kiddies' to him.

«Senza la tradizione non siamo niente»
(Luchino Visconti a Manolo Blahnik nel 1971)

«Luchino Visconti mi ha simbolicamente aperto le porte dell'Italia. Come con una chiave magica. L'ho incontrato, per la prima e unica volta – e abbiamo parlato, in francese – a Londra, in Chalk Farm, alla Round House, nel 1971».
«Perché, Monsieur Visconti, sempre film in costume?» gli ho chiesto. E lui mi ha risposto: «Perché senza tradizione non siamo niente».
Manolo Blahnik, shoemaker extraordinaire, è un appassionato viscontologo da sempre, per istinto o per coincidenza, ancora prima di disegnare scarpe e bottines. E la sua prima creazione – allegrissimi sandali con ciliegie e tralci di foglie disegnati a Londra per Ossie Clark – è infatti parallela al primo incontro con Luchino Visconti.
Visconti ha da allora, e ancora prima (quando, da ragazzo, alle Isole Canarie dove è nato, la visione di «Senso» fu per Manolo una fulminea rivelazione) tracciato una specie di involontario sistema spirituale all'interno del rapporto di Manolo Blahnik con l'Italia. Che è una storia d'amore e di gusto e di fisicità un po' letteraria, ma con molte piacevolezze reali come... le caramelle all'anice a Milano, i garofani in Sicilia (o il distillato di garofano di Santa Maria Novella, a Firenze)...
Tranches de vie, in una specie di trance italiana e viscontiana... il grande vaso di tuberose in «Boccaccio '70» nell'episodio «Il lavoro»... l'amore per Volterra, che è «Vaghe stelle dell'Orsa», così come la Sicilia è «Il Gattopardo» e così come Milano è «Rocco».
Sapori, colori «globali».
«Anche la texture, la materia delle scarpe, fabbricate in Italia, è un'esperienza sensoriale, perché l'Italia è the most sensuous country in the world».
Così, dedicate a Visconti e all'Italia, le delicate scarpe di ottoman ricamato di jais esposte alla Biennale. Ispirate a Romy Schneider nel ruolo dell'imperatrice Elisabetta in «Ludwig», con i meravigliosi costumi del «Signor Tosi», come lo chiama Manolo, raccontano, fuori dal tempo, su un sottilissimo anacronistico tacco metallico di 9 cm, che la moda è soprattutto emozione.
Anna Piaggi

Studiolo di Francesco I
Palazzo Vecchio

Manolo Blahnik

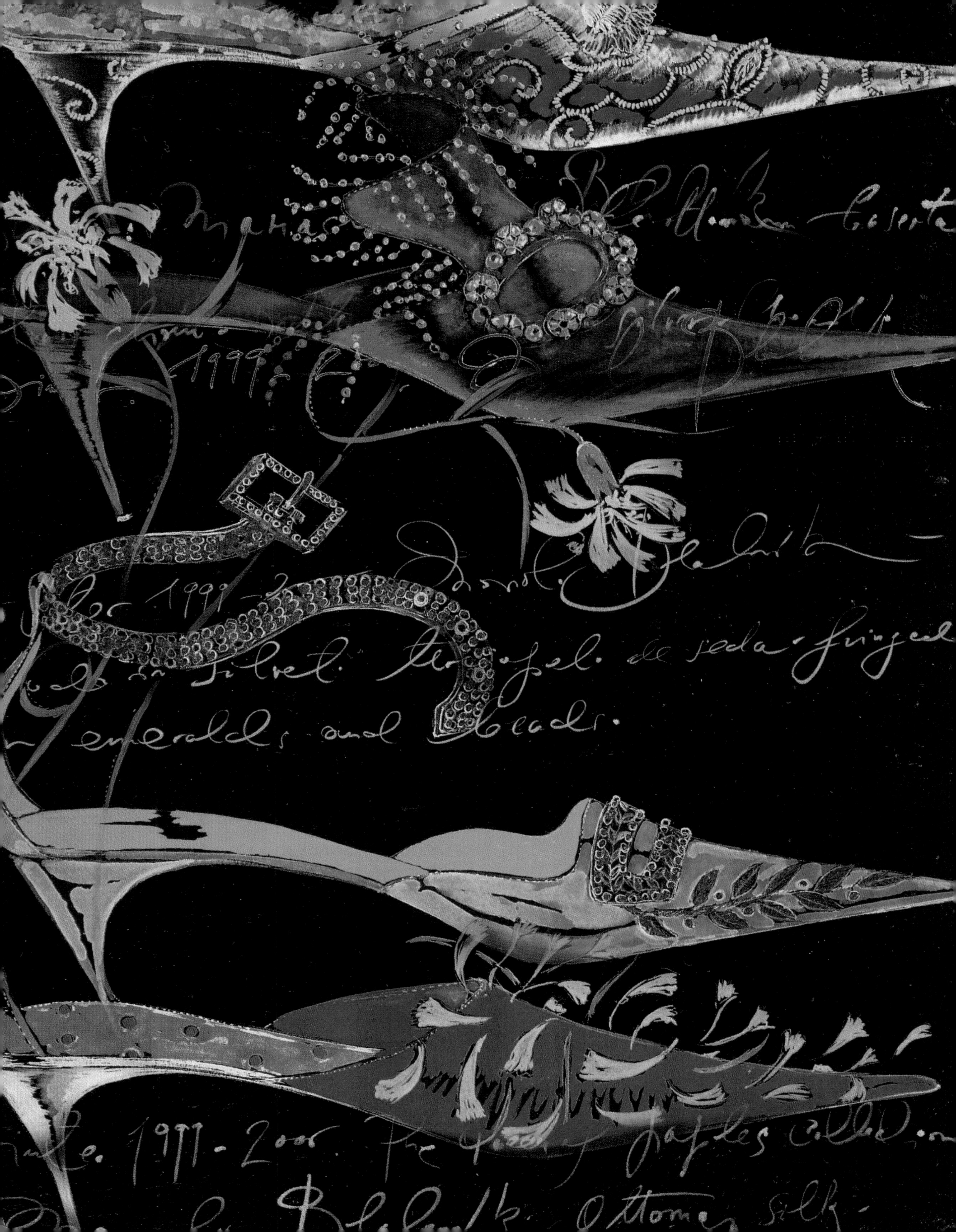
emeralds and beads.
Ottoman silk

'HIGH-GLOSS BLACK LEATHER LOOKS SLICK AND SEXY. AND AFTER A FRILLY SUMMER, IT FEELS SO MUCH MORE POWERFUL'
MANOLO BLAHNIK

Black leather tasselled and belted jacket, £2,825, at Yves Saint Laurent Rive Gauche. Cotton knickers, by Hanro, £11, at Harvey Nichols. Black leather gladiator boots, by Manolo Blahnik for Clements Ribeiro, £435, at Manolo Blahnik.

MARC HOM

Pages 178–179: For the 1997 Art/ Fashion exhibition in Florence, Blahnik's installation echoed Visconti's words in 1971: 'Without tradition we are nothing'. Blahnik celebrated his influences by including a costume worn by Romy Schneider in Visconti's Ludwig, given to him by its designer, Piero Tosi. The catalogue introduction for the exhibit in the studio of Francesco I in the Palazzo Vecchio was written by Anna Piaggi.

Left: Blahnik took the sixties' high boot and reinvented it for the nineties. Ponyskin and tight lacing produce a chic cowgirl look for John Galliano in October 1999 and a gladiatorial, combative look for Clements Ribeiro in August 1997.

Right: One of Manolo's most magnificent inventions of the nineties was this Masai-inspired boot-sandal, which he created for John Galliano's first Christian Dior couture collection in 1997.

He has helped a roll call of international young talent while continuing to design for larger and more established companies. He provides shoes for the Italian firm of Cerruti and, in 1994, signed a contract with the American manufacturer Anne Klein, the label for which Donna Karan designed before founding her own company. Rifat Ozbek, who claimed he loved Manolo's shoes because they were sexually specific, Michael Kors, Todd Oldham, Antonio Berardi, Clements Ribeiro, and Matthew Williamson are just some of the other talents who have also had the advantage of 'shoes by Manolo Blahnik' in their shows. But there are two talents with whom Manolo has had a closer and more creatively special relationship: the New York designer Isaac Mizrahi and John Galliano, the English designer who now works in Paris and is creative director of Christian Dior as well as running his own-name company.

Blahnik's work with Mizrahi began in 1988. Excited by the young American's enthusiasm for the couture of the past, Manolo quickly found that their beliefs entirely agreed on what is important and lasting in fashion: Balenciaga, Norman Norell, Pauline Trigère, the list of shared enthusiasms was long. The other thing about Mizrahi that Manolo found stimulating was his marvel-

lous sense of colour. When he asked the shoe designer to take the traditional and tired men's desert boot and turn this most comfortable of styles into something with the same glamour as his clothes, Manolo jumped at the idea, producing them in the softest of suedes in a glorious range of colours, including pink and violet. They were a sensation.

As were the shoes Blahnik designed for John Galliano's first show for Dior, the couture collection based on the decorations worn by the Masai, intertwined with the designer's obsession with the turn-of-the-century glamour of the grandes dames painted by Sargent and Boldini. 'Think Africa…with a bit of boudoir,' Galliano told him. 'And maybe some Russian…'. It was the sort of brief that ignites Blahnik's imagination. 'I went rushing around Venice, where I was working on the Dior couture collection at the time,' he recalls, 'buying all the beads I could find. Then I rushed back to my hotel with a huge tube of glue and began to stick them on a last to make the sort of thing I had envisaged after John had explained his concept. Luckily, I came up with exactly what he wanted, then John said, "As it's Africa, what about some fur?" I said, "Give me some chinchilla!" In the end they looked like naughty little animals, ready to bite!'

A THOUSAND BLENDED NOTES

Of all the great photographers who have over the years taken on the challenge of photographing Blahnik's creations – and photographing a shoe is much more difficult than other items of dress – it is perhaps Manolo's friend Michael Roberts who has most successfully captured their architectural and sensual quality, as this photograph taken in Sicily in 1999 shows.

He is as familiar with the interior of the palatial Villa Stupinigi built outside Turin at the height of the Baroque as he is with the Guggenheim in Bilbao. He knows the poems of Walt Whitman as well as the latest novel by Gore Vidal. He can tell his Biedermeier from his Bauhaus.

'The Cecil Beaton of contemporary life, Manolo Blahnik, cobbler and interior designer, has a judgement in matters of taste considered impeccable and is much copied, first by the few and then by the many. He is the companion and guide to all seminally chic women in the world, the fiercest of whom will quake in her shoes and prepare to back down on any issue of aesthetics. Although he claims to have no interest in fashion (or perhaps because of it) he is one of the handful of British designers taken seriously anywhere.' The comment of *Harper's & Queen* in 1986 pinpoints the quality that raises Blahnik above other shoemakers: taste.

Blahnik's taste is not the same thing as fashion taste. He has said many times that he hates fashion and dislikes his shoes being considered part of it. Although clearly an overstatement, behind the theatrical denial lies a certain rationality. These shoes are not fashion items. Fashion, by its nature, is transitory and expendable. It requires a seasonal transfusion of new ideas. Manolo Blahnik's shoes are never new in the way fashion views newness. His approach is deeper and more subtle than the mere search for novelty. This attribute he shares with his fellow Spaniard, the couturier Balenciaga, who, asked what new ideas he would be introducing in his next collection, was as bewildered as he was offended and replied, 'New? But I never do anything new.'

What Balenciaga was eschewing was the lurch from one novelty to another that has characterized much of fashion in the past fifty years. He saw his work not as something endlessly changing but something consistently developing along a continuum begun in his earliest days as a couturier. This is precisely how I see the work of Blahnik: always part of the fashion mood of any moment but not in fashion at any specific time. The spirit of his shoes does not change with the seasons. In fact, they have no sense of season. Apart from the obvious variations such as boots being normally confined to winter collections, they are, like the approach of their designer, not merely eclectic but also sempiternal. A Manolo sandal that is two years old is not unfashionable, it is merely an earlier manifestation of a continuing thought process.

Blahnik's oeuvre consists of a series of themes and variations on a highly focused fashion vision. This became clear to me when, in the early stage of research for this book, I went to see his archive. He threw open the doors of the many wardrobes to reveal shelves full of carefully placed shoes covering every season from the seventies to the present day. While Manolo bewailed the fact that there were so many missing shoes (his London shop was disastrously flooded in the late seventies and many shoes were destroyed) I realized what made his work different. There was a constancy of creative purpose in those shoes before us, clearly marking the considered development of an artist-craftsman.

What I was seeing was a physical *catalogue raisonné* of work, showing each little twist and turn of his imagination, each creative

He really should have existed in the brief heyday of late-flowering English eccentricity that flourished in the twenties and thirties. I can imagine how much Lord Berners, the witty dilettante, would have enjoyed Manolo and what an asset he would have been at those Farringdon weekends — a triumph of surrealism over the dreariness of the English countryside — busily helping to dye the doves in pastel colours.

influence, each curve toward a new exploitation of already formalized developments over a career stretching for twenty-seven years. As I worked my way along each shelf, amazed at how undated so many of even the early examples were, two things became apparent. Without any doubt, every idea produced by shoemakers in at least the last ten years has originally come from the imagination of Manolo Blahnik. Further, it was clear that to assess Blahnik's achievement solely in terms of fashion would show only a portion of the picture and risk ignoring the most important part.

It would be nonsense to attempt to see his work in terms of fine art, as Manolo would be the first to admit. Always nervous of pretentiousness and extremely knowledgeable about art, he would be horrified at such an approach. When I first suggested this book to him, he was alarmed and mystified as to who might be interested in it. Although he has been compared by desperate journalists to many artists — Bernini and Michelangelo among them — I believe that is not the route to follow in order to reach the core of Manolo Blahnik's creativity.

Instead, I think his similarities lie with literature: a very particular and specialist form of literature which combines worldliness, scepticism, dazzling phraseology and sparkling wit with an arch, camp awareness on several levels. The writers who come to mind when I think of Manolo Blahnik's work are people such as Thomas Love Peacock and Ronald Firbank. There is more similarity between *Crochet Castle* or *Valmouth* and Blahnik's thinking than there is between him and most people working in fashion. But the man with whom Blahnik has most in common is the pre-World War I satirist, Hector Hugo Munro, who wrote under the pseudonym of Saki. Like Blahnik a romantic, Saki maintained, in the words of the critic J. W. Lambert, 'a scale of values which the modern world has abandoned but still admires'. It could be a description of Blahnik himself.

Saki's stories sparkle with wit and the memorable phrase. His style is chic and sharp, as good fashion is. If there is a fashion equivalent of the memorable phrase then it has to be the witty and precise curve of a Manolo heel, the sharply delineated contour of a Manolo strap and the outrageous irreverence of a Manolo juxtaposition of colour and pattern. Add to it all the big-city sophistication, half world-weary, half excited, of a Dorothy Parker poem — and who would better have captured the louche excitement and vulnerability of a strappy high-heeled 'Manolo'? — and you have the literary antecedents of this most literate of shoemakers. Blend in a touch of the whimsical innocence of A. A. Milne and the knowing humour of Ogden Nash and you have the complete literary parallel to the work of Manolo Blahnik.

But that does not give the entire story of Blahnik's creativity. Surprisingly for many, perhaps, one of his most vivid influences is

Page 187: A Michael Roberts'
photograph in Morocco for Tatler
in 1986.

This page: Sicily, photographed
by Michael Roberts in 1999.

The feet of the old, gnarled, worn and yet perfectly honed by hard work; the feet of an actor such as Ryan O'Neal; the feet of a sex symbol such as Raquel Welch and the feet of a supermodel such as Kate Moss – Blahnik measures them all against the feet of a Greek sculpture, an eighteenth-century statue in the gardens of Versailles or a perfectly proportioned nude by Canova. In his bulky scrapbook of photographs taken on his travels over the years, there are many close-ups of sculpted feet.

Arabic. It began when he was a little boy, finding Casablanca stations on his father's wireless and listening to the singer Oum Kalsoum. He found the music vibrant and full of mental images and he still loves it. Today, he loves Natacha Atlas, who carries on the tradition with a hip-hop, techno beat. It is a reference, like Granada in Spain, Cuba, the poems of Lorca and even the music of Sudan, that has been of paramount importance in his creative and cultural development.

There are other strong and consistent strands to Manolo's approach. Preeminent is architecture, an interest since he was an adolescent. To talk to him about great buildings is to realize that, had he not been daunted by the technical, mathematical elements involved in practical architecture, it is a field in which he could easily have made his mark. It is possible to imagine him as an academic, writing about architecture, but it is much more convincing to visualize him creating delicious follies, temples or gazebos in the mock-Georgian manner of the between-the-wars English designers and illustrators such as Rex Whistler and Oliver Messel.

There are certain historic anomalies we all wish we could put right. As I have come to know Manolo while researching this book I have often wished that I could, in some godlike *legerdemain*, turn back the clock and place him in the ambience that was surely made for him. He really should have existed in the brief heyday of late-flowering English eccentricity that flourished in the twenties

and thirties. I can imagine how much Lord Berners, the witty dilettante, would have enjoyed Manolo and what an asset he would have been at those Farringdon weekends – a triumph of surrealism over the dreariness of the English countryside – busily helping to dye the doves in pastel colours.

Or maybe he would have been happier fighting the philistines, shoulder to shoulder with Harold Acton, enjoying the hidden charms of Norman Douglas's Capri or helping to design a grotto in the garden of La Pietra, Acton's superb villa above Florence, whilst animatedly discussing the Medicis or the Bourbon kings of Naples? Or with William Walton on Ischia, creating a paradise garden? In fact, the people who really would have brought Blahnik to a creative apotheosis were the Sitwells. How he would have enjoyed helping Edith design her jewellery and discovering fresh nuances for her unique and eccentric approach to medieval dress. Who could have talked to Osbert Sitwell about classical architecture with as much authority, or whistled the latest Constance Lambert melody with as much panache as Blahnik?

All designers have their cultural *cachepot* into which they dip, usually subconsciously, not only for inspiration but for confirmation of the ideas, feelings and mood they use to renew their inspiration. Blahnik's is deeper than most and covers a longer time span than that of the average fashion person. He is as familiar with the interior of the palatial Villa Stupinigi built outside Turin at

the height of the Baroque as he is with the Guggenheim in Bilbao. He knows the poems of Walt Whitman as well as the latest novel by Gore Vidal. He can tell his Biedermeier from his Bauhaus.

Maybe Blahnik's Catholic upbringing is responsible for his love of ecclesiastical architecture, from the *quattrocentro* monasteries of Tuscany and Umbria to the churches of Bernini and Borromini, but when he talks about southern Mediterranean churches he becomes a Renaissance man – not in the sense of being all-knowledgeable, but in the sense of understanding the spirit that informs the buildings. This is to do with his awareness of space, of what happens between two pillars or in a corner, away from the light. He realizes that great architecture is not merely about enclosing but also about releasing space. And the eye that assesses a campanile or dome is the eye that judges to the millimetre the space between the toe and the heel of an elegant shoe.

It is not a surprise to learn that, even as a child, it was people's feet that Manolo noticed and remembered. He was aware of the beauty of many of the feet of the peasants working in the banana groves. The feet of the old, gnarled, worn and yet perfectly honed by hard work; the feet of an actor such as Ryan O'Neal; the feet of a sex symbol such as Raquel Welch and the feet of a super-model such as Kate Moss – Blahnik measures them all against the feet of a Greek sculpture, an eighteenth-century statue in the gardens of Versailles or a perfectly proportioned nude by Canova.

In his bulky scrapbooks of photographs taken on his travels over the years, there are many close-ups of sculpted feet.

There are also many of gardens, often out of season, when their bare bones are clearly seen. The anatomy of gardens interests him because the lines and axes remind him of the veins and bones of a well-proportioned foot. Blahnik knows a great deal about gardens, both in theory and in practice. He has visited most of the great gardens of the world. He is familiar with Isola Bella and Bomarzo in Italy; Aranjuez and the Alhambra in Spain; Villandry and Vaux le Vicomte in France and, in some respects his favourites, the gardens of England. He is aware of the subtle difference between a Spanish and an Italian garden and why one in New England is different from its inspiration in old England. Like feet, it is a question of anatomy and proportion.

Manolo Blahnik is an avid reader and one of the genres he finds continually fascinating is biography. He ranges wide, over politics, the arts and the lives of the socially significant. Not surprisingly, given his trade, he is fascinated by stylish women. Not to be confused with the merely fashionable, the women who attract him have had some sway in public life, have made a mark for reasons less transitory than fashion statements. He not only appreciates the great beauties – women such as Lady Abdy, Mrs Dudley Ward or Gladys Cooper – but knows how and why they have changed the concept of beauty in their time.

Blahnik responds to elegance and confidence in women as much as in architecture or sculpture. The appearance of Edith Sitwell interests him as much as the beauty of Pier Angeli. But, above all, it is style that fascinates him. That is why he idolized Diana Vreeland, whose face reflected her personality – wilful, powerful, but with a sweetness for those she liked, which included Manolo. It is also why he admired Jackie Onassis, whose beauty held an iron courage in the face of tragedy, or Diana, Princess of Wales who, behind the ease and charm, had an inner strength masked by what Manolo calls 'a classic beauty which could only have become stronger and more extraordinary had she lived'. Other women admired by Blahnik include Amanda Harlech and Lucy Ferry, both of whom have supported him for years and sum up the kind of strength of personality and confidence of taste that makes designing for British women so rewarding for him.

There is a world inhabited by a particular kind of strong woman which gives the real clue to Manolo Blahnik's creativity. It is a world that brings together many of his interests and influ-

ences. In the visual arts the world of the great shoemaker has most in common with that of the great interior decorator. We can compare him with the silvery precision of the Adam brothers and find much in common. We can read the views of Edith Wharton on decorating and realize that Manolo shares many of them. We can imagine rooms which might have been decorated by Bakst and know that Manolo would be totally at ease with them

The work of a powerful troika closely coincides with Blahnik's. All three were active in the halcyon days before London became 'swinging', a period I have already said is, in my view, the time in which Blahnik should have been working. They are Elsie de Wolfe, Nancy Lancaster and Sybil Colefax. What they had in common, with each other and with Blahnik, was courage, wit and style. More important, they had a delicacy of touch and a sophisticated eye that enabled them to re-create and idealize the past in a way that kept its charm but was entirely modern. Their rooms were entirely of their moment. The skill to mix periods in such a way that they create an entity in themselves, not only of no particular

A Raymond Meier picture for British Vogue, July 1994, captures the flower-like delicacy of Manolo's sandal.

Just as he keeps abreast of literature, the theatre and film, his voracious openness to the new enables him to respond to the work of architects such as John Pawson, Frank Gehry and Rafael Moneo and designers of the calibre of Philippe Starck, Antonio Gaudi and Oscar Tusquets. A cultural polymath, he is aware not only of the past but the present, not merely of the current but also the avant-garde.

moment but making their own moment, is rare and undervalued and this is what makes Blahnik different from other shoemakers. He may well use eighteenth-century marcasite buckles, nineteenth-century *point d'esprit* or Edwardian velvets for his creations, but he does so to create something modern. There is no hint of costume or pastiche in anything that Blahnik does.

And, indeed, why would there be? He does not use his knowledge of past cultures to hide from the present. Even though his understanding of the arts of the past subconsciously informs all he does, his work is as modern and forward-looking as that of any designer, in fashion or industry. It could be no other way. Just as he keeps abreast of literature, the theatre and film, his voracious openness to the new enables him to respond to the work of architects such as John Pawson, Frank Gehry and Rafael Moneo and designers of the calibre of Philippe Starck, Antonio Gaudi and Oscar Tusquets. A cultural polymath, he is aware not only of the past but the present, not merely of the current but also the avant-garde. In our conversations there was nothing creative happening today of which Manolo was unaware – this, after all, is a man who will add a day to a schedule to see an exhibition or change a flight to visit a new building. It is what one would expect from a man who designs modern furniture and dreams of designing an utterly modern, minimalist house for himself of perfect proportions and simplicity, a house reflecting his belief in the logic of all design.

But it is to film that Manolo and I kept returning when we talked – and almost inevitably, to the great actresses of the past.

They are, perhaps, the most lasting influences on Blahnik's creativity because they remain vivid in his imagination. A chance remark, a reference, a picture in a book can spark a memory – and it is a complete one. Time and again, I have been amazed at Manolo's recall of films he saw even as a boy. He usually remembers the theme music, he can invariably describe not just the *mis en scene* but the atmosphere and, inevitably, he can repeat chunks of dialogue. Add to this an encyclopedic knowledge of bit players, B-movies, directors, producers – even best boys and gaffers – and it builds into a formidable cultural arsenal.

I recall driving through an industrial wasteland outside Milan, on the way to a factory with him. It was a chilly, misty morning and the view from the window was the opposite of glamorous. We turned a corner. Suddenly, Manolo sat upright, staring out of the window. All I could see was the scruffy backyard of a small factory, with three small watertowers at the side. 'Look', he cried, pointing, 'Like a Roman amphora.' Within seconds he had launched into a description of an early Sophia Loren film he had seen when he was twelve, which was set in biblical times and had amphorae at various points. He recalled the plot completely, enthusiastically remembering, 'I was absolutely possessed by Sophia Loren. Those wet clothes, as she came out of the sea! In those days on the island the movies stayed only three days. I went every afternoon!'

It is axiomatic that Manolo Blahnik is intensely visual. He creates spontaneously. Unlike many designers, he has no agonies of emptiness when it is time to start thinking about a collection.

And yet, for Manolo Blahnik, making shoes is so all-encompassing and rewarding that, to borrow Shelley's phrase describing the Italy Manolo loves, it combines 'the loveliness of the earth and the serenity of the sky'. Manolo Blahnik is a fortunate man.

He never turns to old magazines or art books for inspiration. He doesn't need to. The inspiration is within him and, as he says, 'It's spontaneous. There's never anything calculated in my stupid brain. I see things and suddenly I remember other things and my memory book is open. Ideas flow out quicker than I can draw them. It's never a question of sitting down and thinking, "What can I remember?" but the reference is always something of the past.'

This can be Manolo's own past, as in the case of movies or his life on the island. Both were such seminal influences that he often wonders, 'Do I romanticize my childhood? I don't know, but all I have is happy memories. We lived a quiet and sheltered life. There was nothing extravagant about it. For example at Christmas, my sister and I were given a book, maybe a cardigan – and it was absolutely enough. Our great joy was the cinema – as it has been all through my life, although I go much less frequently now.' It isn't only because he is under so much pressure that Blahnik has allowed the pleasure of a lifetime to slip away, it is because he finds modern films uninvolving. 'It's the actresses,' he says. 'They're very pretty and charming but they have no substance. Most of them aren't actresses, really, they're starlets. And that's because there aren't parts for big actresses. What would Anna Magnani – or even Tallulah Bankhead – act in today?'

Manolo Blahnik has a personality generally considered larger than life so it is not surprising that he is attracted to women who are larger than life. That is why he is stimulated by the Marchesa Casati, who was painted by Boldini, loved by D'Annunzio and, a social firefly, flitted across Europe in the early twentieth century. Heir to a fortune, she spent it on parties, extravagant living and an outrageous wardrobe and she died alone and without pity, bankrupt. She is to Manolo's taste because she was uncompromising – and uncompromisingly tasteful – in everything she did.

Equally extravagant, financially and emotionally, was Rita d'Acosta Lydig, who is particularly dear to Manolo's heart because of her obsession with shoes. Hers was not the vulgar, uninformed acquisitive passion of an Imelda Marcos, which is of no interest to him. He warmed to Mrs Lydig because she understood the beauty of shoes, the skill of their making and the artistry of their conception. She paid a fortune to Yanturni to handmake them, waiting months and even years for delivery, but once she possessed them she treated them like the minor works of art they were, having specially fitted trunks made of Russian leather for storage and taking them with her wherever she travelled. It was love.

And it is love that drives Manolo Blahnik. Conceiving and creating shoes is his lifelong passion. He becomes tired; he is often frustrated; the process of making can be slow and intractable; some of his most exciting ideas fail to excite the public; he spends too little time at home and too much abroad; he is frequently alone. And yet, for Manolo Blahnik, making shoes is so all-encompassing and rewarding that, to borrow Shelley's phrase describing the Italy Manolo loves, it combines 'the loveliness of the earth and the serenity of the sky'. Manolo Blahnik is a fortunate man.

INDEX

ACKNOWLEDGEMENTS

PICTURE CREDITS

David Bailey, Cecil Beaton, Gilles Bensimmon, Antoni Bernard, Evangelina Blahnik, Eric Boman, Alfa Castaldi, Paolo Castaldi, Carolyne Cerf de Dudzeele, Beverly Chapman, Terence Donovan, Michael Duignan, Linda Evangelista, Torkil Gudanson, Kristina Huselbus, Hywell Jones, Tina Laakkonen, Karl Lagerfeld, Barry Lategan, Peter Lester, Pamela Hanson, Nick Knight, Tiggy Maconochie, George Malkemus, Raymond Meier, Steven Meisel, Sheila Metzner, Anna Piaggi, Jamie Prieto, Michael Roberts, Johnny Rosza, Paolo Roversi, Peter Schlesinger, David Seidner, Mario Testino, Bruce Weber, Tony Yurgaitis.

Manolo Blahnik would also like to thank: Maia Baudet, Marisa Berenson, Sandra Bernhard, Katherine Betts, Angelica Blechschmidt, Isabella Blow, Tina Brown, Holly Brubach, Joan Juliet Buck, Guillermo Cabrera Infante, C. Garcia-Calvo, Naomi Campbell, Graydon Carter, Daniella Cattaneo, Lucinda Chambers, Tina Chow, Grace Coddington, Ronnie Cooke Newhouse, Loulou de la Falaise, Anna della Russo, Carrie Donovan, Marianne Faithful, Lolo Fernandez, Lucy Ferry, Amy Fine Collins, John Galliano, Jerry Hall, Amanda Harlech, Petra Hartman, Anna Harvey, Sarajane Hoare, Cathy Horyn, Iman, Bianca Jagger, Ninivah Khomo, Marguerite Littman, Elsa Lopez, Maribel A. Lugo, Madonna, Cynthia Marcus, Amada Matos, Patrick McCarthy, Polly Mellen, Suzy Menkes, Beatrix Miller, Kate Moss, Sarah Mower, Jacqueline Kennedy Onassis, Rifat Ozbek, Molly Parkin, Walter Pfeiffer, Kate Phelan, Paloma Picasso, George and Elizabeth Pochman, Phyllis Posnick, Candy Pratts Price, Colombe Pringle, Carine Roitfeld, Elizabeth Saltzman, Elissa Santisi, Marina Schiano, Stephanie Seymour, Alexandra Shulman, Irene Silvagni, Lord Snowdon, Carla Sozzani, Franca Sozzani, Mimi Spencer, Amy Spindler, Janet Street Porter, Tilda Swinton, André Leon Talley, Burt Tansky, Elizabeth Tilberis, Oscar Tusquets, Diana Vreeland, Sheila Wetton, Anna Wintour, Iain R. Webb, Veronica Webb, Linda Wells, Lynn Wyatt, Peter Young – 'and my greatest thanks to my mother'.

Endpapers: Paolo Castaldi: 4: Alfa Castaldi; 6, 9: Michael Roberts/Maconochie Photography; 12–21: Manolo Blahnik; 24: Antoni Bernard; 25: Cecil Beaton, from Manolo Blahnik private collection; 26: Alfa Castaldi; 27: Peter Lester; 29–32: Manolo Blahnik; 35: David Seidner, from Manolo Blahnik private collection; 38–41: Manolo Blahnik private collection (unknown photographer); 42 Manolo Blahnik; 43: Barry Lategan, from Manolo Blahnik private collection; 44–7: Manolo Blahnik; 48: Peter Schlesinger; 49–50: Manolo Blahnik; 51: Johnny Rosza, from Manolo Blahnik private collection; 52–75: Manolo Blahnik; 78: Steven Meisel, courtesy of Barneys; 80: Manolo Blahnik; 81: Courtesy of *Interview* magazine; 82: Manolo Blahnik; 83: Pamela Hansen, courtesy of *Vogue* USA; 84: Marc Hispard, courtesy of *Vogue* USA; 85: Carlyne Cerf de Dudzeele; 86: Oberto Gili, courtesy of *Vogue* USA; 87: Walter Chin, courtesy of *Vogue* USA; 88: Pascal Chevalier, courtesy of *Vogue* USA; 89: Raymond Meier, courtesy of British *Vogue*; 90–1: Raymond Meier, courtesy of *Harper's Bazaar*; 92 (left): Michel Arnaud, courtesy of British *Vogue*; 92 (right): Gilles Bensimmon, courtesy of *Elle* USA; 93: Karl Lagerfeld, courtesy of *Vanity Fair*; 96–124: Michael Roberts/Maconochie Photography; 125: Manolo Blahnik; 126–9: Michael Roberts/Maconochie Photography; 130–7: Manolo Blahnik private collection; 138–149: Michael Roberts/Maconochie Photography; 150–5: Manolo Blahnik; 157: Michael Roberts/Maconochie Photography; 160–1: David Bailey, courtesy of British *Vogue*; 162–3: Michael Roberts/Maconochie Photography; 164: Manolo Blahnik; 165 (left): Mario Testino; 165 (right): Harry Peccinotti; 166–9: Manolo Blahnik private collection; 170 (left): David Bailey; 170 (right): Lothar Schmid, courtesy of British *Vogue*; 171 (left) Michael Williams, courtesy of *Harpers & Queen*; 171 (right): Terence Donavon, courtesy of British *Vogue*; 172 (top left): Eamon J. McCabe, courtesy of British *Vogue*; 172 (top right): Oberto Gili, courtesy of *Vogue* USA; 172 (bottom right): Steven Meisel, courtesy of *Vogue* Italia; 173: Nick Knight, courtesy of *Vogue* Paris; 176 (left): Bruce Weber, Manolo Blahnik private collection; 176 (right): Eric Boman, Manolo Blahnik private collection; 177: Nick Knight, courtesy of British *Vogue*; 178: Catalogue of Florence Bienale; 179: Manolo Blahnik, courtesy of *Vogue* Italia; 180 (left): Matthew Donaldson, courtesy of Russian *Vogue*; 180 (right): Marc Hom, courtesy of British *Vogue*; 181: Mario Testino, courtesy of *W*; 184: Michael Roberts/Maconochie Photography; 187: Michael Roberts/Maconochie Photography, courtesy of Condé Nast; 188: Michael Roberts/Maconochie Photography; 190: Sheila Metzner, courtesy of *Vogue* USA; 191: Sheila Metzner, courtesy of British *Vogue*; 192–3 Hywel Jones; 194: Raymond Meier, courtesy of British *Vogue*; 197: Torkil Gudanson, courtesy of *Vogue* Deutsch.

First published in the United Kingdom in 2000 by Cassell & Co

A CIP catalogue record for this book is available from the British Library

ISBN 0 304 35411 2

Design Director David Rowley
Designed by Kate Stephens
Edited by Tim Cooke
Printed and bound in Italy

Cassell & Co
Wellington House
125 Strand
London WC2R 0BB